kayak morning

also by roger rosenblatt

kayak morning

REFLECTIONS ON
LOVE, GRIEF, AND SMALL BOATS

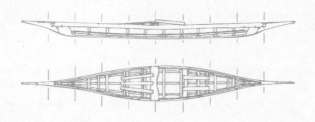

roger rosenblatt

ecco
An Imprint of HarperCollinsPublishers

FIRST EDITION

Designed by Suet Yee Chong

Library of Congress Cataloging-in-Publication Data
has been applied for.

ISBN 978-0-06-208403-3

12 13 14 15 16   OV/RRD   10 9 8 7 6 5 4 3 2 1

For my family

kayak morning

Two and a half years after our thirty-eight-year-old daughter, Amy, died of an undetected anomalous right coronary artery, I have taken up kayaking. They say that people in grief become more like themselves. I have always been a loner, so going out in a kayak suits my temperament. It also offers a solitude that is rare for me these days, because when Amy died, my wife, Ginny, and I moved into her house in Bethesda, Maryland, to help our son-in-law, Harris, care for their three small children, Jessica, Sammy, and James. We spend nearly all our time in Bethesda, but we have also kept our home in Quogue, a summer village on the south shore of Long Island. It is not far from Stony Brook University where I teach English and writing. I commute between Bethesda and Quogue from September to June, and from

June to September in Quogue, whenever time allows, I go kayaking.

Our oldest son, Carl, and his wife, Wendy, also have three children, Andrew, Ryan, and Nate. The family spends much of the summer together in Quogue, as we did when Amy was alive. When I am more sure of myself with my kayak, I will take the kids out with me one at a time, sitting them between my legs as I paddle. "It would be cool to see the water from the water's point of view," says Sammy, a serious-minded child. Early in the morning, I go out by myself.

It is Sunday, June 27, 2010, just past dawn. At home, everyone is asleep, including our youngest son, John, who is visiting for the weekend. My boat scrapes on the public ramp. I dig my paddle into the pebbles in the shallow water, and push off.

———

Past a wooden dock jutting out into the creek and littered with parts of seashells, strafed by gulls. Smashed china on gray boards. Past the skeleton of a fish bobbing in the suds near a tuft of sea grass, thick as a sheep's head. Past the orange buoy and the wet brown sand. A neap tide settles like a defeat. The sky is a blue stripe, squeezed between two wide layers of white clouds. Over the canal it turns gunmetal gray. Elegies of water. Could rain.

———

I try to be careful about kayaking. I bought a good, sturdy boat, olive green. I got instructional books and took a couple of lessons. I have learned to sit straight and to hold the paddle with my hands between its center and the blades. I bring a bottle of water if I am to be out awhile. I spray on sunscreen. I wear my PFD, a life vest now called a "personal flotation device." I rarely paddle farther than ninety feet from shore. Amy would have approved of such preparations and precautions. As a child she would pore over toy instructions. As a wife and mother, she read booklets on household appliances from cover to cover. As a pediatrician, she was tirelessly careful with her research and with her patients.

Until recently I was never like that. I thought I could figure out everything as I went about it, and simply plunged in. When I was eleven, our sixth-grade teacher, Miss Washburn, asked if anyone in the class played a musical instrument. She invited us to perform the following day. My aunt Julia had just given me a guitar for my birthday, on the day of Miss Washburn's invitation. So I decided to bring in my new guitar even though I had not a single lesson in the instrument and had not even touched one until that day. The following morning, I stood in front of the class singing "Red River Valley" to the one major chord I'd figured out the night before. My classmates were shaking and screaming with laughter. I must have thought that playing the guitar would simply come to me, like a miracle.

———

You can't always make your way in the world by moving up. Or down, for that matter. Boats move laterally on water, which levels everything. It is one of the two great levelers.

———

Where I go is Penniman's Creek, an inlet shaped like a wizard's hat, squiggly on the sides and bent at the point. Not far from my home, the creek is about two hundred yards wide at the mouth, and a half mile long, one of several creeks leading from the village to the Quogue Canal. The canal leads to Shinnecock Bay and Peconic Bay, which extends east to Montauk at the tip of Long Island, and into the Atlantic. I venture no farther than Penniman's Creek, paddling up to where it meets the canal, and then paddling back to the narrow end. Not much of a trip, if measured in distance covered. Nothing, as compared to the Atlantic, which hooks into the Pacific. Nothing, as compared to the Pacific, which is sixty-four million square miles. With more practice and confidence, I eventually shall go into the canal and the bays, perhaps even as far as the ocean. For now, Penniman's Creek is my Atlantic and Pacific, quite big enough for me.

———

Still waters, dark waters, watercolors, waterproof, watermark, high-water mark, waterbird, to be in hot water, brackish water, white water, water main, water lilies, waterworks, waterfront, water bug, water cannon, water table, watershed, dead in the water.

———

The duck squats sits unmoving, a gray-brown shack. I've never seen it used. Retired hit man, it sits with straw popping out on all sides in the wrong places, like old men's hair, thirty yards or so from the marshes and the shore on the east side of the creek. Above it rise trees of a hundred greens, thick as privet hedges—bright green, purple green, green descending to black, pale green, nearly white. White oaks, willows, pitch pines, tupelo trees whose branches stick out at a ninety-degree angle. One dead tree, the color of ashes, rises among them like a corkscrew. The trees are tall where the creek comes to a point and grow shorter and sparser where it widens at the canal. Three or four solitary trees appear on the promontory, at a distance from one another. One is flattened at the top like the desert date trees I saw in Sudan in 1992, when I was writing a story on the "lost boys" for *Vanity Fair*. Half hidden in the foliage are houses, summer places, most of them sprawling with additions. One of the larger houses has a flagpole on its lawn. I read the wind by the American flag flapping and clanking against the pole. Big houses. Substantial and confident houses. The creek rolls to them and away.

Elsewhere, great herds of bathers soon will gallop on the nearby ocean beach, calling out to one another in loud, patrician voices and complaining about a slice of swordfish scorched on the grill last night. They will organize their lives into committees under yellow-and-white beach umbrellas, while the sea rears up against its reins. On the creek I am the crowd—I and the birds and the insects and the fish. Beneath me lie the gothic rocks in their dark museums. The minnows move in fits and starts. The banded killifish explode upward like sparks from a bonfire in the evening.

Powerboats ride at anchor on the west side of the creek,

halfway between the canal and the public ramp. They belong to members of the Shinnecock Yacht Club, founded in 1887, merely a smallish house and a dock with a few slips. There are nine boats anchored in the creek today. None is oversize or showy, thus all are showy in the way of Quogue, which often makes a vice of modesty. The boats are still, as are the egrets that congregate on the dock. They stand together but seem not to acknowledge one another. It's difficult to determine their policy.

On the rocks above the public ramp, a rust-brown dinghy lies upside down, looking like a sea lion lolling in the sun. Nearby, a bush presents a small bouquet of pink and violet flowers. J. M. Synge had a phrase for such a picture— "the splendid desolation of decay." The pilings of the various docks stick up like periscopes. The sky has turned gray and white, white clouds rising into the gray. The moon leaves a trace, as a chalky eye. White the pebbles. White the tips of the waves. White the weeds. Birds wheeling in the wind. The screak of gulls.

———

"It colors everything I do," I said.

"What did you expect?" said my friend.

"I'm in a box."

"Isn't that what grief is?"

"You're the doctor. You tell me."

"What do you want?" she said.

"I want out."

"What do you really want?"

"I want her back."

"Well," she said, "you'll have to find a way to get her back."

———

Back at the house, everyone should be awake by now. Sammy, Jessie, Andrew, Ryan, and James are blasting one another with water-shooting Max Liquidator Styrofoam tubes. Carl, John, and Harris are comparing notes on last night's Yankees game and the World Cup. Ginny and Wendy are sipping second cups of coffee, while Nate, having recently learned to walk, makes his way from chair to chair around the kitchen. Ginny gathers up the towels, pails, and shovels to prepare for a morning at the beach. James tires of warfare and plays with his red dump truck. The boys get on their trunks and swim shirts. Jessie goes to the piano and plays "Beauty and the Beast."

Opposites attract me. In kayaking, taking the opposite way can save your life. When you feel you are about to capsize, you instinctively clutch the gunwales of the boat. You think that the kayak offers stability on an unstable surface. But you are part of the boat when it rolls, and grabbing the sides merely adds mass to the problem. You must use your paddle to support the boat, extending it into the water and holding it facedown, because in this instance the water is more stable than the boat. And, to do this maneuver correctly, you have to lean into the paddle, which will put you off balance. When you are completely off balance, so much so that you are certain you will topple over—you bring the paddle down hard on the water's surface, the way ducks bat their wings. You will feel your kayak right itself. Only by moving in the direction you least trust can you be saved.

⌣

Anomaly. Deviation or departure from the normal or common order. Peculiar, irregular, difficult to classify. Aberrant.

⌣

No one has a heart like yours . . .
—LINDA PASTAN, "ANOMALY"

⌣

Cloud-ghosts pass along the skull of the sky. Two gulls wheel by together. A single-engine plane drones eastward. Purposeful little bugger, it makes a beeline. The sun is a blur, a slowing pulse. The water looks shellacked. I poke about at the shore, where the creek has worn lines in the rocks. The rocks bear evidence of the creek. If the creek should dry up, the rocks would know it existed. The moon slides out of sight, in its secret night. I am contained in my boat. Form rescues content.

————

They say that you can lose yourself in nature. I spent much of my New York childhood doing that, wandering off one path or another on hikes led by grown-ups, and scaring them shitless. At age seven, I strayed from a walking tour of Central Park led by one of our neighborhood parents, having decided to make a walking tour of my own. I wound up in the park police station. In Cape Cod, at the age of three, I wandered away from my parents' rented summer cottage and headed for the beach, where I played with dead horse-shoe crabs. The police were called then, too. Holding a crab at my side, I watched the lights of the police car bouncing toward me on the hard sand.

A curious phrase, to lose yourself. Like the word *given*

in reference to prison sentences. When you're given a year, a year is taken from you. Similarly, when you lose yourself in a book, you've probably found yourself, as you have when you're lost in your own thoughts. I hated school. During class, I would daydream out the window at one bright leafy tree. "Roger," a teacher would call to me. "Would you like to rejoin the group?" I thought, *Not really.*

Some years ago in Paris, French farmers staged a protest against the government by transporting sheep, cattle, and pallets of wheat to the center of the Champs-Élysées. Police braced for the outbreak of fights between the Parisians and the farmers. But when the citizens caught sight of the sudden farms arisen in the middle of the city, their reaction was to stroll in the fields—lovers, farmers, policemen, rediscovering the companionability of the countryside, as well as something basic in themselves. I dream into an egret preparing her morning lecture on the information explosion. Miss Egret regrets.

⁓

We regret to inform you.
We are pleased to inform you.
We beg to inform you.
We refuse to inform you.

We are devastated to inform you.

We are tickled pink to inform you—pink, and a becoming pale yellow, too, and a fetching shade of sage.

We are afraid to inform you, frozen in fear, actually, to such a degree that we may never inform you.

We could not inform you if we wanted to. We have informed you of everything. There is nothing of which you remain uninformed.

⁓

The news blares stories about the oil spill in the Gulf. Reporters grill BP officials. The company president says he wants his life back. Fishermen say their lives are as good as gone. Oil puddles on the water, like mercury. Pictures of oil creeping to the shore. Pictures of sea turtles, dead in their tracks. Pictures of brown pelicans, blackened as if tarred. Tarred and feathered. A seabird so laden with thick oil, it looks ossified, a purple-and-gray stone bird. Its head is glazed, its eyes closed, as if in prayer. One can barely look.

Weather people report that the spill could curl around the tip of Florida and worm its way up the East Coast, past Alabama, North Carolina, the Maryland Eastern Shore, New Jersey, New York, into the bays below Long Island, then to the canals and the creeks. A cormorant alights on a rich man's dock. It teaches nothing.

———

Nature is neutral. On September 26, 1827, Goethe said to his friend Eckermann as they sat together on a grassy slope, "I have often been on this spot, and of recent years I have felt that this might be the last time that I should look down from here upon the kingdoms of the world and their glories; but see, it has happened once again, and I hope that even this is not the last time that we shall both spend a pleasant day here. In future, we must often come up here." The two men were enjoying a picnic at Buchenwald.

That stand of pines at the narrow end of the creek. It has no use for me. It occupies its own world, not mine— aliens grown from seed. I carry no wallet with me in my kayak, no cell phone either, no photo ID. I could lose my paddle and disappear without a trace, drifting past the pines toward the bays and the ocean. Not one tree would blink. The nameless soldier in *The Red Badge of Courage* flees like a coward, feels shame, peers up and sees the sun as a bright wafer in the sky—the way it appears right now.

———

When you're in a small boat, everything feels big except yourself. Above me rise the houses on the creek, with their solid docks and their several boats—sailboats, powerboats, rowboats, zodiacs. The pilings and the bulkheads tower over me. I am smaller than everything I observe, like a cartoon mouse or, smaller still, a mosquito plying my way through the halls of giants. At any moment, a barefoot woman in shorts, smart and stylish, could saunter from one of the houses, poke her big toe in the water, and cause a tidal wave, upending my kayak and drowning its tiny pilot. I call out for help, but my voice is too small.

———

All I have to keep me afloat, all I have ever had, is writing. In 2008, I wrote an essay in the *New Yorker* about our family after Amy's death. A year later, I expanded the piece into a book, *Making Toast*. In it, I tried to suggest that the best one can do in a situation such as ours is to get on with it. I believe that still. What I failed to calculate is the pain that increases even as one gets on with it. The response to the book indicated how many others have experienced similar losses and feelings. I have received nearly a thousand letters from people telling me their stories and wishing our family well. The letters keep coming. Everybody grieves.

A woman approached me on the street in New York. I had never seen her before. "I read your book," she said.

"I'm sorry for your loss," I said.

———

Be kind, for everyone you meet is carrying a great burden.

—ATTRIBUTED TO PHILO

———

Sunday morning. And churchgoing Quogue is as quiet as the grave. Impossible not to think of "Sunday Morning." Such a strange poem. The ambiguity of the title. Wallace Stevens on the inadequacies of a Christian conscience. His two ladies, his wife and his dying mother, aloof and untouchable, but oh-so-pious. Everything and everyone, unattainable. The past, unattainable. And the importance of Sunday morning, associated with going to Sunday school and going to church. He needed to understand the women in his life. He needed to believe. All these themes swimming about in the complex poem. Yet for the reader, the images are plenty—"Complacencies of the peignoir, and late / Coffee and oranges in a sunny chair, / And the green freedom of a cockatoo." I do my thinking with my senses.

Here, the ducks whettle out in their crazy syntax. The swans sail by with mud on their keels. The tides rummage with the pebbles. The sunlight hones the edges of the whited houses, etching guillotine blades on the walls. What I liked about Stevens was his rage for order. Things as they should be. Everyone in his place.

———

Objects I never intended to see take on disproportionate significance. The gull's stone eye. The heron's wobbly legs. A jellyfish suspended like an open parachute just below the surface of the water, the red veins in the chute. A tassel of seaweed attached to a log. And the log itself, blackened, drifting toward my kayak. It looks like a swimming dog. I cannot tell if I am seeing the whole thing or a portion of it. I wallop the waves. The log creates a weir. I swerve in one direction. The log swerves in another, as if it were steering intentionally. See? It edits itself. The creek is a palimpsest lined with corrections.

Kayaking is like writing, requiring the same precision and restraint. You are definite, stabbing the paddle blades into the water. Wild swings will get you nowhere. Writing requires generosity toward every point of view. Kayaking insists on all points of view—the water's point of view, as

Sammy observed, and that of the birds and of the sky, and of the algae and of the insects. Writing is for important things, matters of substance. There is no point in going out in a kayak unless you feel the potential profundity of the act, the adventure that opens before you. You are alone and not alone. No one writes alone. Write, and you are in the company of all who have written before you. No one paddles alone.

———

Why do I kayak? I like the rhythm of paddling
and the feeling of being out in the open water,
responsible for and in control of my actions. The
sensation of freedom under the big sky, separated
from solid ground, and the three-dimensional
movement accentuated by wave and swells. When
one is completely immersed in the elements,
experience is heightened as increased awareness is
demanded and dulled senses are rejuvenated.

—WERNER FURRER SR., *KAYAKING MADE EASY*

———

If Icarus fell over there in that obscure corner of the creek— the winged ankle of Brueghel's painting and of Auden's poem, sticking up from the black water for a moment before it disappears—I'd probably notice. In Auden's mind that would make me alert to amazing things, and not blind to suffering, as were the townspeople in the painting. They went about their townspeoply lives. They did not care about the falling figure. I'm on their side. Who was Icarus, after all, but a reckless boy who stole his father's car? The people of the town had work to do. They functioned in the real, hard world, not among stars. "About suffering they were never wrong, / The Old Masters," said Auden. Suffering? A hotdog show-off who made a little splash?

Painters are attracted to boats because boats are beautiful and imperiled. J. M. W. Turner painted a typical masterpiece with a very long title: *Snow Storm—Steam-Boat off a Harbour's Mouth Making Signals in Shallow Water, and Going by the Lead.* He wrote: "I did not paint it to be understood, but I wished to show what such a scene was like; I got the sailors to lash me to the mast to observe it; I was lashed for four hours, and I did not expect to escape, but I felt bound to record it if I did." The painting is pure Turner, blending funnels of browns, tans, and whites assaulting an indefinite boat and its frail, tall mast. Turner was Melville's favorite painter.

Albert P. Ryder, of the Hudson River School, based a painting on Chaucer's "Man of Law's Tale," in which Constance, daughter of the emperor of Rome, and her infant son are cast adrift by the emperor's enemies, without sail or rudder. Miraculously they survive and eventually are guided back to Rome. Ryder believed in God's protection. In the painting, Constance appears to be calling out for help, and she has nearly disappeared in the blankets that cover her and her child. The brown boat seems to float in a dead calm on the green sea. Above it are layers of clouds that could be seen as either threatening or comforting. When you look at Ryder's painting, even if you do not know Chaucer's story, you feel assured that mother and child will find their way home.

It goes without saying that the banded killifish is covered with bands, and he also bands together, which makes it difficult to approach him individually. But I try, letting my kayak drift to the little crescent beach beyond the Yacht Club as noiselessly as possible. The killifish are undisturbed, at least by me. They seem preternaturally disturbed by themselves, twisting in gangs like striped kites in the wind. Wall Street traders in a panic. There's one. Odd to say that. There's one. He's just like all the others—same eye, tiny mouth, tail, bands. Stick him in a police lineup, and he'd swim away scot-free. The more I stare, the more he stays the same. Does he regret his lack of individuality? Was there ever, in the long distinguished history of killifish, an Emerson among them who built his reputation on saying such things as "Whoso would be a killifish must be a nonconformist"? Was he admired? Was he shunned?

Caught swimming in a riptide once, I learned to drift. I dream a different picture from the one around me. The sky sinks into the creek. The creek geysers up, looms over the trees in a reverse waterfall. The seabirds tear at one another with their beaks, revert to eggs, and burst into flame. A great red wing, twenty feet across and shaped like a knife blade, rises from the bay. The sun sheds darkness. Nature out of order.

———

"You have to understand," she said. "Grief lasts forever."

"Like death," I said.

"Like death. Except death is someone else's condition, and grief is all yours."

"I feel worse now than I did shortly after she died."

"And you'll feel even worse next year. And worse the year after that, unless you find a way to transform your grief."

"We're back to that."

"We've never left it," she said. "Grief comes to you all at once, so you think it will be over all at once. But it is your guest for a lifetime."

"How should I treat this guest? This unwelcome, uninvited guest."

"Think of the one who sent it to you," she said.

———

A kayak is a small, narrow boat in which you sit at the center and propel yourself with a double-bladed paddle. Some kayaks are open on top, some have decks fore and aft with a cockpit in the middle. They come in various shapes. Some have symmetrical hulls. Some have the Swede form, with a large bow and a narrow stern. The fish form has the opposite shape. The bows vary as well. A traditional bow looks like a dog's snout and rides with a great deal of buoyancy. A vertical or plumb bow is rounded at the tip. It cuts through waves rather than rides on top. The Greenland looks like a shark, flaring high in the water and offering a high ride at the expense of a short waterline. Keels also vary, from a straight line to a slight rocker. Most kayaks have a shell made of fiberglass or polyethylene plastic or wood. All are swift, silent, and built for solitary progress. My father was a kayak.

My mother was a rowboat, tied to a dock and bobbing gently. When she was young, she was beautiful, quick witted, and sharp in her 1940s dresses. She taught junior high school English in a public school on Hester and Baxter Streets, on New York's Lower East Side, where she and my father were born. She played the mandolin. She played chess. She made ceramic plates and vases. Everyone said, "Hello, Molly!" when she and my father took their Sunday promenades in our Gramercy Park neighborhood. "Hello, Doc." "What's new, Molly?"

In the early stages of her Alzheimer's, not long after my father died, she was still alert enough to her disease to recognize when she wasn't making sense, and was often amused by it. Ginny and I took her to lunch at the Gramercy Park Hotel. "We ought to do this again, soon," I said, as we were about to finish. "Yes," said my mother. "But the next time we come here, we should invite Joseph Cotten." Ginny and I searched each other's eyes to try to determine what my mother meant. No one in our family knew Joseph Cotten.

"Why do you want to ask Joseph Cotten, Mom?" I asked.

"Because Joseph Cotten can tell precisely what part of the country you come from by your dialect."

I asked her if she was thinking of Rex Harrison in *My Fair Lady* or Leslie Howard in *Pygmalion*.

"Yes," she said. "I was thinking of Rex Harrison." She gave us a little smile. "But as long as we've already invited Joseph Cotten, I don't think it's right to renege."

A white glove floats into view and bobs beside my boat. It seems lit from underneath. Its condition is pristine, as if a wind had swept it off the counter at Saks or Macy's and blown it out to sea. Now it comes to me, bright white, looking like Mickey Mouse's glove, or the glove that minstrels wore, Al Jolson singing "Mammy," or a group of careless young things painting the town red in the Jazz Age. It might have belonged to one of the people who used to attend Jay Gatsby's parties. Edgar Beaver. It might have belonged to him. Or to Gatsby himself—the glove he wore those nights he beat oars against the tide.

TWA Flight 800 went down in Moriches Bay not far from here. The crash rattled the roof of our house, eight miles away, as if a giant's hand had given it a shake. East Moriches fishermen had gone out in their boats in an effort to rescue survivors. Soon they saw it was hopeless. "I prayed I wouldn't find a kid," one of the guys told me. "Then I found a kid." Some days later, I walked the beach in Quogue. The detritus of the plane had washed up on the sand. I found a fragment of a red merino sweater enmeshed in a dark knot of seaweed, an imitation alligator skin eyeglass case, a watch, a doll, and a toothbrush as good as new. I reach down to touch the white glove. The fingers are swollen and waterlogged. They feel like parsnips.

On the other hand, somewhere in Quogue at this moment a family unknown to me is pedaling their bikes on the road to the beach, duck fashion. A mother and father in the lead, with three kids behind, the youngest pumping as hard as he can to keep up. When they arrive, they park their bikes in the racks. Then, with the kids running ahead and hollering, the parents mount the wide, white wooden steps up the dune, two at a time. When they reach the top, they remark upon the ocean—how it goes on forever.

Tolstoy said, "The biggest surprise in a man's life is old age." Not really.

At the end of Claude Brown's *Manchild in the Promised Land*, he recalls his childhood and the unbelievable yet real things that went on in the streets. "You might see someone get cut or killed," he writes. "I could go out in the street for an afternoon, and I would see so much that, when I came back to the house, I'd be talking and talking for what seemed like hours. Dad would say, 'Boy, why don't you stop that lyin'? You know you didn't see all that. You didn't see nobody do that.' But I knew I had."

Those years I wrote about the world: the laughing old Red in Moscow who wore a formal white shirt and bright blue sweatpants, with his bald head wrapped in a bandage fastened by a safety pin. He had seen Lenin at the Finland Station. And Trotsky. And the czar, in 1913, at a celebration of the three hundredth anniversary of the monarchy. "He stood thirty meters away!" The handsome old woman in Iowa, with a biting tongue, who had been a friend of Amelia Earhart's and had seen her off on her final flight. The Brooklyn father who beat a rolled newspaper on the head of his six-year-old son, to force him to learn to read. "See?" he said. "Smart." The fifteen-year-old Belfast girl who saw her mother shot to death on the street, caught in a cross fire between the Protestants and the IRA. The eight-year-old Cambodian boy whose father was executed by a firing squad before his eyes, and who later had to bury his mother beside him. The eight-year-old Cambodian girl who was forced by Pol Pot's soldiers to participate in the beheading of another child. In the refugee camp in Thailand, she would not speak for a year. The two airmen who presided over nuclear missiles aimed at Moscow, underground in a silo in Great Falls, Montana. They looked like teenagers. A Diet Pepsi rested on the console. The homeless woman who sang for pennies on the streets of upper Broadway, schizophrenic, dying of emphysema, who claimed to have been Miss Cincinnati when she was young, and to have danced in the chorus line at the Latin Quarter, and to have dated Joe DiMaggio—and she was, and did, and had.

The patients in the Beirut mental hospital—Lebanese, Jews, Maronites, Shi'ites, Druze, Sunnis, Palestinians— crawling on the cement floor in their own excrement and smelling of urine; the legless girl who spooned mush into the mouth of her little sister; the flame-haired woman who lunged at me and shouted, "I am normal!" The Hutu man squatting in the door of his tent in Tanzania a few days after the slaughter in Rwanda, who grinned at me and drew a line with his finger across his throat. The museum director in Hiroshima who, as a schoolboy when the Bomb was dropped, ran around the city shouting, "Is there anyone alive?" The young woman with melancholy eyes, who posed for a street artist on Nevsky Prospekt in what was Leningrad. In her hands she rolled two plums. She never smiled. When the artist was done, she paid her rubles, and without looking at the sketch, tucked it carefully under her arm and disappeared in the darkening afternoon, among the women and men in coarse overcoats, into an underpass.

———

But I knew I had. Ayen, a woman of twenty-three, lived under a tamarind tree in Nimule, Sudan, near the Ugandan border. She spent most of her time sitting on a green tarpaulin folded at the corners. Both her children were dead from malnutrition. Her husband was "away." Day and night Ayen lived under her tree, surrounded by her possessions—a tin cup, a plastic bottle of water, a plastic bottle of oil to mix with sorghum. Behind her lay a covered orange plastic bowl of tamarind nuts, bitter but rich in vitamin C, and a few large tins used for washing. In the crook of the tree, where the trunk split into an array of branches, Ayen stored extra clothes and rags. But for her shaved head and the incessant coughing, she might have been mistaken—in her blue dress on the green tarp—for a young woman on a picnic.

"What do you think about under this tree?" I asked her.

"Nothing," she said. Her coughing drove the flies from her lips.

"Do you think about your children?"

"No."

"What do you do?"

"I dream."

What do you dream about?"

"Nothing."

No man is an island, but I do my best. Never exactly smooth in social situations, lately I have become so much worse. I sympathize with anyone burdened with my companionship. At a dinner party the other night (Why did I go? Why did they ask me?), I was seated between two women. The woman to my right I have known, episodically, for thirty-five years. Her husband is a political journalist. I asked her if he was still writing. "Don't you read the papers?" she said. I told her I do not. I then turned to the woman on my left, whom, for the entire evening, I called by the name of the woman on my right. The two women might as well have been seated beside a hedgehog.

Such occasions bother me less (not at all, in fact) than the lack of attention I give my friends when we get together.

I listen, and I nod. But I am not "in it," as one is in a kayak, for example. I sometimes feel that death is contagious, that I could pollute others with my sorrow. It is a lot to ask of people to add your despair to their own. Because my friends love me, they understand and forgive my deposed state of mind. I recognize the kindness in their eyes. When they suffered deaths in the family, I saw the gauze over their faces. Now they see mine. I sometimes feel that I betray them, being out of things. More often, I feel ridiculous, like a hedgehog.

Whereas the social life of the creek is busybusy. The double-crested cormorant has no oil on its feathers, which allows it to dive deep for bunker fish. Or it stands with its wings spread wide like the Angel of Death, and watches. Everything chases something else. Bluefish drive shiners into shallow water. Their location is noted by the snowy egret. The great egret. The great blue heron. Such stature. The mud bulges, throbs. Killifish congregate near the shore. They are prey to blue claw crabs, which are prey to crows, gulls, and us. Everything lives here. A man I know found a seahorse clinging to a rope on his crab trap. Fluke and flounder in the creek. Dragonflies and damselflies that pull back their wings when they land. Crows that caw, mob, and dive-bomb the northern harriers and marsh hawks and osprey that threaten them. A pair of osprey is building a nest at the mouth of the creek. The barn swallows and the purple martins feed on insects that feed on us. The mussels look asleep, but they siphon the water of microorganisms. Snakes, rabbits, and mice on the prowl. Trees crack and tumble. Muskrats gnaw at the stumps. Even the plants are busy. Vines called bitter-sweet open into bright orange stars and glom onto bushes. At night, if you're lucky, the comb jellies will light your way and glow like music in the dark.

Look. The creek lives. The household you left lives. Your husband, children, your brothers, friends, the kids' teachers, your old professors, colleagues, patients, the store clerk at Nordstrom, the Terminix man. Your mother. Me. Look. I've been calling your name. Your name lives.

———

Surprised by joy—impatient as the wind
I turned to share the transport—Oh! with
    whom
But Thee, deep buried in the silent tomb,
That spot which no vicissitude can find?
Love, faithful love, recalled thee to my mind—

But how could I forget thee? Through what
    power,
Even for the least division of an hour,
Have I been so beguiled as to be blind
To my most grievous loss?—That thought's
    return
Was the worst pang that sorrow ever bore
Save one, one only, when I stood forlorn,
Knowing my heart's best treasure was no more;
That neither present time, nor years unborn,
Could to my sight that heavenly face restore.
—WILLIAM WORDSWORTH, "SURPRISED BY JOY,"

SONNET ON THE DEATH OF HIS DAUGHTER

The literature involving fathers and daughters runs to nearly one thousand titles. I Googled. *The Tempest. King Lear. Emma. The Mayor of Casterbridge. Washington Square.* Daughters have a power over fathers, who are usually portrayed as aloof or mad. The father depends on his daughter, and he is often isolated with her—the two of them partnered against the world. It is a good choice for writers, this pairing. It may be the ideal male-female relationship in that, with romance out of the picture, the idea of father and daughter has only to do with feelings and thoughts. Unalloyed. Intelligent. A girl may speak the truth to her father, who may speak the truth to her. He anchors her. She anchors him.

———

Amazing things, anchors. An anchor may weigh twenty to thirty pounds, yet it can secure an eighty-foot ketch weighing ten thousand pounds or more, pulling its weight against a chain in a storm. Certain boats need anchors, and anchors need boats, or they would have no place in the world.

But a kayak would not be a kayak if it had an anchor, because the kayak wants *you* to be responsible for its security, its stability. An anchor can hold a ketch to a stop. A kayak can never stop, unless you employ a technique with your paddle, and even then it's up to you. Everything about a kayak is up to you. The point of the craft is that there is nothing beneath it but water. The creek is the anchor. You are the anchor. Unreliable creek. Unreliable you.

———

Annie Dillard, who knows a thing or two about creeks, admired how light skitters on the water. Creeks, she said, presented her with a different side of nature. Heretofore, she had seen nature as solid and slumbering: "The world abides." When she looked into Tinker Creek, however, she saw nature as a marketplace, alive with coming and going. My Penniman's Creek bears her out, with its battalion of cygnets, and its dragonfly cartel, and its own skittering light.

And Gary Snyder said: "When creeks are full / The poems flow / When creeks are down / We heap stones."

And Raymond Carver said, "I love creeks and the music they make." Me too. Great rivers get all the attention. You can't stand in the same river twice. Ol' Man River, he just keeps rollin'. Riverrun. And a river runs through it. The language of rivers is deep and philosophical. Not so with creeks. Creeks are simpler creatures. They exist to flow into other things and are sources of enlargement. They are destined to become something else, something bigger. "It pleases me," said Carver, "loving everything that increases me."

———

Creek. mid-15c., creke "narrow inlet in a coastline," from kryk (early 13c.), probably from O.N. kriki "nook," perhaps influenced by Anglo-Fr. crique, itself from a Scandinavian source via Norman. Slang phrase, up shit's creek, from Pawnee Indians. Reference to the

Republican River which was polluted with buffalo manure. In deep trouble.

———

James was home with strep a while ago. I thought I'd caught it from him. Sore throat, headaches, fatigue. He was well in a matter of days. But with me, the antibiotic didn't take, and the symptoms persisted and multiplied. The headaches grew worse and more frequent. The throat, inflamed. I developed canker sores. My voice was weak. For the first time in my life there was weakness in my legs. When I started to stand, I had to hold on to something solid to pull myself up. I had to take a crap after every meal, though the meals grew less frequent. I wasn't hungry. I napped three or four times a day and slept like death at night. I slurred my words. I had shortness of breath, especially when I carried little James up or down stairs.

Ginny made an appointment for me with our doctor and insisted that I present him with a list of all my symptoms. "Don't shoot the breeze with him, as you always do," she said. "Tell him you're sick." The doctor looked at my chest, my glands. He gave me two separate blood tests, to cover the bases. The results came in the following day. "Not only is there nothing wrong with you," he told me on the phone. "You're in near perfect shape. Your white count is good, blood pressure good, heart good, cholesterol good, PSA as low as can be. On paper you're as healthy as a horse." I held the receiver and listened. "Are you depressed?" he asked.

⌣

When you love someone, every moment is shadowed by the fear of loss. Then loss occurs, and you feel more love than ever. The more you loved, the more you feel the loss. Depression, then, may be seen as the strongest expression of love. That's where logic gets you.

⌣

"Yet I have learned to live with my grief," said Milosz. Good for you, Czeslaw. But I still squirm in the barber's chair, shaking my head in disbelief, while the barber says, "Can't you sit still?"

⌣

In Rwanda, I saw the Kagera River. In Ireland, the Liffey and the Irish Sea. In Iceland, the Baltic Sea. In Latvia, I walked along the hard, wide beach on the Black Sea. In Israel, I read a newspaper while floating on my back in the Dead Sea. In Hong Kong Harbor, I spoke with children who had fled Vietnam by sailing up the South China Sea. I went to Tinian in the western Pacific Ocean, the tiny island that served as the airfield from which the *Enola Gay* took off for Hiroshima. In Suriname, I took a dip in a river in the company of piranhas. In the Galápagos, I played with sea lions. They swam between my legs. In the Caribbean, I went snorkeling. In Wyoming, I went fly fishing in the Snake River. I've seen the Thames, of course, and the Loire, and the Danube, and the Volga. I've sailed in Maine, in the Atlantic, have taken a container ship from Cyprus to Beirut, in the Mediterranean, and a ferry on the Mississippi, and have ridden in a tribal canoe in the Amazon. I have paddled a kayak on Penniman's Creek.

GRAND CONTESTED ELECTION FOR THE

PRESIDENCY OF THE UNITED STATES

WHALING VOYAGE BY ONE ISHMAEL

BLOODY BATTLE IN AFGHANISTAN

—HERMAN MELVILLE, *MOBY-DICK*

Something about the water makes you feel alone, even when you have company. Isolation at sea. Jefferson envisioned the country aborning as a population of landed gentry living on vast estates, each one positioned at great distances from the others. He might as easily have seen America as a flotilla with high-masted sails, and one captain alone on each vessel. We bob along in solitary confinement. The dark loneliness of this country remains belowdecks. Hawthorne and the nineteenth-century Romantics had us pegged. So did Perry Miller, Puritanism's great scholar. I paddle my boat on my small errand into the wilderness, bearing the rolling liquid weight of the nation.

So many others have gone this route. In August 1732, officers aboard the *St. Gabriel*, a Russian ship anchored off the Seward Peninsula in western Alaska, spotted "a leather boat which had room for but one man." It is the earliest description of a kayak, later embellished by a naturalist on an expedition led by Vitus Bering, the Dane who gave his name to the eponymous strait. He described Aleuts paddling kayaks made of hides stretched over animal skeleton parts—skin and bones. Two hundred and eighty years ago, and possibly for four millennia before that, the kayak was a tool, not for recreation but rather for fishing and hunting. Non-Aleuts use it for similar purposes today.

My brother Peter tells me that he counters grief's isolation by speaking to Amy every day. I have known others over the years who also have talked to their beloved dead. It must give comfort, these one-way conversations. I do it too, but I do not expect that Amy listens. Were I to think that, it would suggest that she is in some place of contentedness, prepared to receive visitors. My daughter is not peaceful in death. She would have refused the undertaker's arm, slapped it away. Blood of my blood, she is as angry as I—angrier—unable to reach those she loves. She would rend death with her teeth.

I prefer to think they cannot hear us. That makes speaking to them more of a challenge, like communicating with the deaf, but without the aids of sign language or lipreading. The art of conversation is severely tested in such a circumstance. The protocol confused. Like talking into a wind that blows your words back at you as soon as they are uttered. I'll make up something: we can talk to the dead but they cannot hear us, save on one day a year, when everything we have said in the previous year collects and assaults their ears in a torrent of gibberish. And, alas, that day is the very same day on which the dead choose to speak to us, and they would do so, except for the din.

⌒

What is the difference between grief and mourning? Mourning has company.

⌒

"Something in you has to change," she said.

"I'm too old to change. No, I take that back. I would not change if I were young. I've never changed."

"It's time. You need to believe things you've never believed in."

"I'm not submissive."

"You'd better learn, or you'll turn to stone," she said.

"You've noticed," I said.

"You're hopeless."

"That, too."

She paused. "You need to change."

⌒

An old man has lived alone on Quogue Street, not far from us, all the years we have been here. During that time, he has had three dogs as companions, yellow labs and black labs. When one dog died, he found another. He was tall and lanky, and a bit stooped, yet he moved quickly for his age, in long, sure strides. On his twice-daily walks he talked gruffly to his dogs, and encouragingly too, and he patted their heads. I used to see him when I walked our terriers. We would wave or nod briskly, as men do. We never spoke. It has been months since I saw him. I think he's dead, I don't know why. The dog, like the hound in Piero di Cosimo's *Death of Procris*, sitting beside the body of his fallen mistress.

Burt Lancaster played a dying old man in a movie made in Quogue some years ago. I can't recall its name. I think it was Lancaster's final role. The man he played had gathered his extended family around him during his last days, and the movie is about that—the interrelationships and the history of the family and the reconciliations to be made. After the old man dies, his grandchildren lay him in a boat they have built, a model of a Viking funeral boat. He had asked to be buried that way. They set the boat on fire and haul it out to sea. On the whole, the movie wasn't much. But that image—of the body and the boat in orange flames on the blue ocean—was memorable.

Crazy old men in boats: Coleridge's Ancient Mariner. Hemingway's Old Man. Captains Ahab, Nemo, MacWhirr, Wolf Larsen, Queeg, Bligh. Barking loonies absorbed in their wild searches at sea, so driven by their fanatical dreams, they pass by themselves along the way. The water is indifferent.

Cold. It does not care if the old men find what they are seeking. It would as easily support them as drown them.

———

Nautical news from overseas: A Dutch boat builder, Johan Huibers, has constructed a Noah's Ark, in the exact proportions indicated in the biblical plans. Huibers's ark, made of cedar and pine, is 150 cubits long, 30 cubits high, and 20 cubits wide. That is, 65 yards long, and as high as a three-story house. Inside, he has placed life-size models of giraffes, elephants, lions, crocodiles, zebras, bison, and other animals. On the top deck, he plans a petting zoo, with lambs, chickens, goats, and a camel. Huibers, a creationist, hopes that his ark will "renew interest in Christianity" in the Netherlands. He does not suggest exactly how that might happen.

One more craziness committed in God's name, for God's sake. Harmless enough, though it may backfire for Huibers, as it reminds the Netherlands of the story of Noah's Ark. God, fed up with human behavior, sends a flood so that he may give the world an extreme makeover. A frustrated writer tosses his first draft. What's the lesson of this parable? The petulant child throws a fit and destroys the flawed creatures whom he deliberately made flawed. The world in the hands of a temperamental artist. Now, that's original sin.

⁓

See here, Amy. There's little point in making mistakes unless you make the same mistakes over and over. One wants
to get good at it. The trick is to recognize and seize the
opportunities. I have had so many close calls, when I had
a habitual mistake in the palm of my hand and nearly let it
slip away. Experience helps. With you, on the other hand, I
did the right thing once in a while. My behavior improved
from time to time. Occasionally I was impressive, someone
to look up to. Clearly I was not myself. You were a disruptive
influence. Now who is there to lead me astray?

⁓

The mudbank is rank with four dead blue claw crabs, stuck
in the mud like junked jalopies. I inhale the rich smell. Deep
brown mud embedded in itself, looking like the knobby
heads of small animals. Or gourds. Or mold. Or clumps of
turf. Yes, that. Turf. Turf fires. And Ginny and I living in
Ireland for a year when I was a student there. And going
to plays nearly every night at the Abbey and the Gate. And
drinking in pubs afterward, with other students and the
local poets, drunk as lords, and cultivating a taste for Jameson's, until Ginny was pregnant with Carl.

And the obstetrician who said, "No charge. Americans have been very kind to me. Just send a picture when he's born." And the postman who covered his mouth with his hand whenever he had to pronounce our name. Our name. And the book auction, where we won a bid on *At Swim-Two-Birds* and other books, and they couldn't understand "Rosenblatt" when I called it out, and wrote on the package of books, "Frozenwhemm."

And Connemara, and the outcroppings of rocks on the beach, and the hard sea. And learning enough Irish Gaelic to curse the weather in a dozen different phrases. And Dublin. And the painted doors of the nineteenth-century houses. And the solemn quays. And the long walks in the gloaming. And the shopkeepers who tossed superannuated pianos in the Liffey. And lingering conversations with people you've only just met. And playing basketball for University College, Dublin, against the Garda, the cops, on a slate court. And visiting the poet Austin Clarke with his piles of books on the floor and his rich, dusty world. And a picnic in Carlow, sitting with our friend Niall Montgomery near a creek like Penniman's, when all was ahead of us—Carl, Amy, John— all of life ahead. And taking classes with Frank O'Connor at Trinity. And reading Sean O'Faolain, who said that "and" was the most hopeful word in the English language. And.

———

Niall Montgomery knew Joyce in the last years of Joyce's life. He said that Joyce could not accept the idea that people are base, have dark sides and dirty thoughts. Joyce, of all people, could not abide such talk. "We're all animals," Niall said to him. Joyce shuddered at the thought. Had he realized he'd covered life with one brief moment in his story "Clay," written when he was eighteen years old, he never would have cringed at the idea of being human. The moment belongs to Maria, the irritating and lonely old woman who is preparing to spend Halloween with the family that has no use for her. She is in her little room, dressing for the evening. She puts on her blouse, her skirt, her shoes. She studies her tidy little body in the mirror. She readies herself to face the outside. Is there more to life than this?

———

Sitting in Starbucks the other morning, reading Pat Barker's *Regeneration,* I found myself at a table beside two men in conversation. Both were in their forties. One was interviewing the other for a job, something in real estate. The would-be employer was large, with thick shoulders and a murmuring voice. The applicant was fat to the point of obesity, but he was neatly dressed in work pants and a purple-and-yellow-checkered shirt. He had a huge head, with watery eyes and a dark brown mustache and a short thick beard. He'd brought along a copy of his résumé. He explained why he had been let go at his last job. The first man said "uh-huh," and described what the schools were like in the area. Near the end of the interview, he made it clear he had nothing that suited the applicant's qualifications at the moment, and even if something opened up, it would pay only fifteen dollars an hour. The applicant nodded rapidly as the other spoke. He understood how things were, he said. And, for his part, he wasn't going to take any old job that came along. "I'm looking for the right opportunity," he said.

———

These endless embraces. In coffeehouses, in shopping malls. In Chuck E. Cheese. Teenage girls. Athletes on the field. Boys in the 'hood. Women friends and men friends. I think the practice began in the early 1980s, about the time "bottom line" seeped into usage. Everyone seeks the bottom line. Everyone embraces. Antipodal cultural impulses—at one end the shame, at the other the apology. The florist embraces me. The people at the market as well. I embrace a student I hardly remember. The Toyota man approaches me with open arms.

———

In the throes of one thing we feel the other. We know our fall even as we rise. What is the opposite of grief?

———

Only literary jerks like me think of *Moby-Dick* in Starbucks. Seeing the world through a book darkly. I'm not sure it's good for you. A group of us English graduate students used to eat in a diner, where we always were served by the same waitress. She was tall, with black hair and a lyrical voice. One day she asked what we were studying, and we told her the Romantics. "Oh," she said, "I'd love to read that!" So we gave her a book of Byron. She returned it a day later. "I don't get it," she said. "Where's the romance?"

And yet there was Leon Wieseltier, shortly after Amy died, giving me an annotated version of Wordsworth's *The Excursion.* I'd skimmed the poem in graduate school, but never attached it to my life. For a year I let the heavy volume sit on my desk, knowing Leon would not have given it to me had he not determined that it would matter. Leon reads the soul. And then one afternoon, when the Bethesda house was quiet and the children still at school, and I alone, I opened the poem to Book Four, taking in the lines: "One in whom persuasion and belief / Had ripened into faith, and faith become a passionate intuition." I may have been without religion, but I used to have faith. Now I was without faith and belief and persuasion, too, and thus without passion. I read the lines and saw where I was.

Keats wrote of Fanny Brawne, "Everything that reminds me of her goes through me like a spear."

———

The good die first,[*]
And they whose hearts are dry as summer dust
Burn to the socket
—WORDSWORTH, *THE EXCURSION*

———

And. And the night of your birth, with the Harvard police driving us to the hospital, and you popping so fast, Mom hardly knew she was in labor. And the white blanket they swirled you in, and the little hospital bed, and so much hair, and such big eyes. And my Modern Poetry class applauding at the announcement of your existence. And the Dunster

---

[*]   "This will never do."
        —*Edinburgh Review*

House tower lit in your honor that night, glowing like the yolk of an egg.

———

Before Billy Budd makes his presence known on the warship *Bellipotent*; before he impresses Captain Vere with his self-lessness and his courage; before he wins the affection of his new shipmates and enrages Claggart with his virtue; before Claggart goes mad with envy of Billy; before Billy kills Claggart, who dies to bring Billy down; before Billy is hanged in the name of a purposeless justice; and long before he looks up into the night sky and loves the stars . . . before all that, when he is still a merchant seaman aboard the *Rights-of-Man*, the ship's master tells the lieutenant who is about to impress the impressive Billy: "Lieutenant, you are going to take my best man from me, the jewel of 'em all." From that moment, as any reader can tell, Billy is doomed, which is the way doom makes itself known, at least in books. The mere statement of innocence presages its passage. Claggart's envy is a signal.

———

The thing about literature, students . . . Are you paying attention? The thing about literature is that you know when something's coming. Always there are signals. Anticipation trumps surprise. In life, however . . . I scare easily these days. If someone comes up behind me when I am lost in thought and cannot hear their approach, I jump. Have even screamed.

Last week, in Chautauqua, I had a public conversation with Marsha Norman. She has a new play about the Sioux in 1890. It centers on the Ghost Dance, a religious movement developed at the time of the Wounded Knee Massacre, in which U.S. Army troops killed over one hundred fifty Lakota Sioux. The Ghost Dance was also a ritual to raise the dead. Marsha said the Sioux had a saying: "The dead are just one song away from the living."

Zombie movies. *Night of the Living Dead. White Zombie. I Walked with a Zombie.* I see them differently now. If I could raise the dead—my way, so that there would be none of the googly eyes or the dragging steps, so that you looked and talked and joked as you always did—I would gladly walk with a zombie. There are nights I stare into the dark, listening for the rustle of a branch. Did I write that? Am I the dead one?

Hook me in the gullet. Gut me. Slice me down like the earth's meridian, from north to south. Lay my bones outside my skin.

—

Must be close to eight o'clock. How long have I been out
here? Two hours? Three? Thoughts come to me on their
own steam. Must be my magnetic personality. No. The
kayak is the draw, like the jar in Stevens's "Anecdote," placed
in Tennessee to civilize the slovenly countryside. It didn't do
the trick. Neither does my boat. All things accrue to it for no
purpose and with no consequence. It organizes the universe
the way art organizes the wilderness—without improving it.
We pass the time. Time passes us.

You wonder: if no one had invented time, would everything happen all at once? Maybe that would be a good thing.
Truncated time would relieve us of expectations, and nos-
talgia, too. All of life would be accordioned like the paper
sheath of a drinking straw, and no one would add a drop of
water to open it into a writhing snake. We might still lead
our lives as we do now. But we would not be aware of time's
passing, which means that we would not be aware of death.
There would be presence and there would be absence, and
nothing in between.

Is that how dogs feel when they show such ecstasy at our
coming home after we have been away? Their excitement
is often explained by their not knowing if we ever would

come back. When we do, it is all tongues, tails, and ears. But maybe dogs simply live without time. That way they never know that something can be different later, or that it was different in the past. That way they never know that time is not on their side. I am powerless in everything that matters.

———

What we are. What we cannot be. What we want. What we don't. What we question. What we accept. What we remember. What we forget, or remember too late. What we did. What we did not do. What we fear. What we brave. What we create. What we destroy, that is, kill. What we had. What we lost. What we are. What we were.

———

In the Quogue Wildlife Refuge, they've got a great horned owl in a big, dark cage. He perches in the back, looking like a man who never leaves his men's club. He naps and waits for night, opening an eye from time to time to check out the curiosity seekers who come to look at him. Not a rabbit or squirrel among them. He closes the eye again. A dead white mouse droops across a raised pole in the cage, like an old sock. It's just skin now. The owl would rather be out here, where the creek is, free to do his thing. You don't see many owls in the daytime. But at night they open their great wings and wheel across fields and the woods, taking soundings. They fear nothing.

I saw one as I was driving back from Bethesda one night last winter. The radio was blasting Sting. The owl ignored me. He had killing on his mind. The one in the cage, to whom white mice are delivered like room service—does he still feel like a killer? Or is his life so changed that he no longer thinks of himself as he once was—no matter how many people, not to mention the sign on his cage, assure him that he is indeed the great horned owl.

Water in winter is different. The boats leave it alone—creek, bay, ocean, as ghostly as a deserted summer town. Quogue winters long ago were known for shipwrecks. On January 21, 1897, the *Nahum Chapin*, a three-masted schooner, went down off the beach. Men from the nearby rescue station harnessed themselves to the lifesaving apparatus, but the gale winds, measured at 51 miles per hour, were too much for them, and for the crew on the ship. At 6:30 A.M. the hull lurched, and the masts were sent reeling into the gale. Two of the men in the rigging lost their grip and were tossed into the surf. One more heave snapped all three spars, carrying away the jibboom and the remaining men on board. Nothing was left of the *Nahum Chapin.*

Melville ends *Moby-Dick* with Ishmael bobbing on a coffin in the middle of the ocean. Riding his strange little vessel, he exists on the margin of a shipwreck. He is about to be rescued by the *Rachel,* named for the one who wept for her children.

———

I have carried the coffins of others, and I have spoken at wakes and memorial services. I'm good at it. I have a gift for death. Or had. It never surprises me when I am asked to give a eulogy for someone I hardly knew. One acquires a reputation. I would not speak at your funeral, of course. Yet I participated in the activities beforehand—the choice of the funeral home, the choice of the music, the obit. In the showroom where the coffins were on display there was a tacit competition for selection. The grandest mahogany with ornate carving and brass handles. The simpler boxes, like Shaker furniture. Even coffins test one's taste. The coffins of others I helped to carry—what I remember is the weight, the heft. It is surprising, like a baby's body, how substantial they are. And you have to be careful, as a pallbearer, to maintain the coffin's balance, lest it tip.

Coffin, coin, coif, in, on, con, if, off, no, fin, *fin*. Waiting for anything—an appointment with the doctor, my turn in line at Safeway—I try to focus on a word on a sign or on the front page of a newspaper, and see how many other words it contains. Or I think of one of the children's names. James, of James Solomon, for instance, contains the names of all three children—James, Sam, and JES, Jessie's initials. James Solomon contains many other words. Solo, solemn, some, one, someone, nolo, mojo, jam, mess, mesa, lasso, moon, loon, loose, moose, noose, nose, soon, no, slo-mo, *mon, nom*, not, on, to, mono, so, moss, salon, saloon, ale, lemon, salmon, seal, lea, elm, sale, slam, lo, ol', mean, male, mole, lame, loam, loom, mom, lass, less, lose, loss, S.O.S., amen.

Words mixed with water lose their bite. They do not help. Old words, or new, now, they do not help. I had believed otherwise. If you could say it, or write it, if you could give shape and expression to it, clarity and precision to it, then something good would come. Now I skim. I flip my words. They spin me into silence, all my light and darkness wordless. My therapist friend would tell me that it's all for the good, like righting a kayak by deliberately putting yourself off balance and nearly toppling into the creek. Like the post-war jet pilots who, trying to break the sound barrier, crashed when they pulled the wheel back but sailed through when they pushed the wheel forward. Skipping similes like stones.

———

Gulls alight on surfaces only briefly. They bend their heads to the side like tragic actresses and move on. Fly up like shrapnel. They do not trust the earth.

Too much is made of the value of plumbing the depths. The nice thing about kayaking is that you ride the surface, which is akin to dealing with the task at hand. Hamlet's problem was that he asked too many questions. If he'd knocked off Claudius and his mother as soon as he got home, he'd be king today. Of course he would have missed the play.

Quiet. Quiet beyond quiet. The snakes and eels slither away from me, making not a sound. My boat makes no sound in the listless water. Two swans riding their reflections make no sound. A sentinel duck remains motionless on a bulkhead. The dead trees, quiet. The flight of an egret, quiet. You can't remain still on the creek. The water always takes you some-where. Everywhere I look is a canvas, a Hockney, a Hopper.

Several years ago, in SoHo, a young art student unfurled a painting of the sea for me. She had taken it from the back of her car and was about to set it up on the street and offer it for sale. But I told her I'd buy it on the spot. I wanted it as a birthday gift for Ginny. The painting is six feet by four feet. The top half is one shade of bright blue, the bottom half another, with a blue-black line dividing the halves. The sky merges with the sea. The sea merges with the sky.

Ginny and I have always taken to water. When we were dating in high school, we used to meet at the subway stop on Fourteenth Street and Union Square on weekends at seven in the morning and ride the train to Jacob Riis Park in Queens, where we'd spend the long day at the beach. We baked in the sun and dived in the waves. When we were married and living in Cambridge, Massachusetts, we would drive north to Crane Beach, or just sit together by the Charles River. When we spent the year in Ireland, we chose to go by boat, one of the smaller Cunard ships, the *Sylvania*. When the children were babies, we would take them to whatever beach was nearby. I used to haul a wooden playpen, plop it on the sand, and cover it with a sheet like a tent, to shield them from the sun.

I splash as I swim. Ginny swims silently, like an otter. Amy was the family's best swimmer. As a child she was fearless, running straight to the ocean as soon as we hit the beach. Not far from here, in Southampton, I plucked her from a wave when she was three. It was great luck that I saw her as the wave was about to swallow her. A second is all it takes.

I was not responsible for everything. I did not bring about Hurricane Katrina. I had nothing to do with the spread of smallpox or the Black Plague. The Chicago Fire? I was nowhere near Chicago at the time. Come to think of it, I wasn't born yet—not in time for the Chicago Fire or for the Johnstown Flood or for the San Francisco Earthquake or for the Fall of Troy. Not one of those events can be pinned on me. On the other side of the ledger, I wasn't responsible for the Renaissance, either. Or for the Age of Pericles or the Enlightenment or for Velázquez or Vermeer or Beethoven or Mozart or Michelangelo or Giotto or Dante, when it comes to that. I was responsible for the lives of four other people. That's all I was responsible for. Clinging to memories like pitons. What am I trying to recall?

Whenever winds are moving and their breath
Heaves at the roped-in bulwarks of this pier,
The terns and sea-gulls tremble at your death,
In these home waters.

—ROBERT LOWELL,
"THE QUAKER GRAVEYARD IN NANTUCKET"

The mind is like a kayak.

That's a simile, all right. But what do you mean?

The mind is like a kayak. It prods and pokes about.

Very good. Anything else?

It points. Also travels in circles.

Excellent. The mind is like a kayak.

You're making fun of me?

Not at all. You're king of the similes. Only I was wondering . . .

Yes?

Does it alter the creek?

A bone of solace, waiter, please? My father told me of a time when he was a young doctor, waiting for a train at a country station. Two young men in a convertible tried to make it across the tracks as the train approached. The wheels caught and spun. The train hit the car straight on, leaving the young men crushed in their seats. As my father hurried to them, they were talking as if something minor had occurred. They apologized for the accident. My father surmised that when the train hit them, endorphins were released to block their agony. The young men chatted away, and then they died.

The wake from a cigarette boat in the canal hits my kayak like a rock. I should have seen it coming. But I was looking up at a storm cloud, which ought to have passed by now. It seems stalled, but of course it moves.

I am beginning to give away my books. To Carl, John, Wendy, and Harris. To an old friend's daughter who loves Irish literature. I have known her all her life. To the daughter of a new friend, who has just discovered Thoreau and is about to graduate from high school. To a friend's son who is teaching in a school that has no library. To the Quogue Library. To my students. Novels to some, history and biography to others. Heavy coffee-table art books, and one very small book, four by four inches, of Shakespeare's plays. The goings-on that used to transpire on my bookshelves—sweaty lovers, madmen, murderers, kings—have grown tranquil of late. My books have become mere decorations, and it is time to give them away.

Perhaps it is time to give everything away. Clay jars and prints and paintings. A softball glove. An antique wooden shovel. My writing chair. I can no longer recall when they meant anything. Let them go, as e.e. cummings said about the cheap and malicious people in one's life. Let them go. Let the house go. This year or next, we will sell our home—to a young family, I hope, who will open the door, hug on the threshold, and smile at the start of good things. Amy studied to be a doctor here. She and Harris were married here. Here we sat at the dinner table and ribbed one another without mercy, especially the old man. The old goat. One year, Amy's birthday gift to me was a sonogram, vague and cloudy, floating like a boat in the amino fluid. She was pregnant with Jessie.

"The difficulty in being a child is that children have no power," I said.

"That's not true," said Jessie. "We have the power of thought and the power of kindness."

———

The children I saw in the various war zones spent much of their time staring out windows. I first saw the Vietnamese children in Hong Kong huddled at the grate of a second-story window in the cinder-block apartment house that had been converted to a refugee camp. In Belfast, children perched at the windows of the terrace houses, sizing up strangers who were wandering around their barbed-wire neighborhoods. In Sudan, the huts, or tukuls, had open doors that served the children as windows, as did the doorless tents in the UN camp in Tanzania, for the children of the Hutus and the surviving Tutsis. The same scenes occurred in Israel and Lebanon—children with their elbows resting on the sills, surveying their worlds from house windows, or from bus windows, or from trucks.

Had I asked any of them what they were seeing from their windows, they probably would have said "a tree" or "a street" or "a hill"—any polite deflection to a grown-up's question. More likely they were not seeing anything, but were peering through or past the life around them, ahead of them, and behind them. Their impossible, out-of-control life, framed by a window.

———

If you're happy and you know it, clap your hands, because you're way ahead of the game. And there's something to be said for the perseverance of the itsy bitsy spider, as well as the weasel who went pop. Just be aware that from time to time the bough is liable to break, Humpty Dumpty will fall, London Bridge will fall, all will fall down. Nonetheless, you will notice that the wheels on the bus do go round and round, and when you row row row your boat merrily down the stream, you might come across my Bonnie, who lies over the ocean, and if you do, will you bring back my Bonnie to me?

———

To water everything returns. Larvaceans with their mucous nets. The comb-shaped jellies, and the barrel-shaped salps. A thirty-foot siphonophore, a shovelnose guitarfish, a grouper using its pectorals as oars. They return. A chambered nautilus returns, as does a cuttlefish that disappears in the smoke of its own manufacture. Silver sardines rehearse their synchronized swimming routines. A school of mackerel returns to gleam in the light. At the aquarium in Monterey, California, I saw the *Vampyroteuthis infernalis*—the vampire squid from hell. Its head was dark pink. Its eye was blue—no ordinary blue, but the first blue ever, the blue that defined the color, the blue open eye of the sea itself. It saw everything and into everything, year after year in its cycles.

The Kemp's ridley sea turtle, which measures twenty to twenty-eight inches in length, weighs from eighty to one hundred and ten pounds, and has a heart-shaped shell, makes a fetish of returning. The turtles come here in late summer. They start out in Mexico, on a single stretch of protected beach near Rancho Nuevo, Tamaulipas. Seabirds swoop down on the eggs. The turtles that survive swim north, all the way to Long Island, where they learn to eat spider crabs. When they are ready, they swim south again, into Chesapeake Bay, where they dine on full-size crabs. Then back down to Mexico, where they lay the eggs. Imagine being programmed to do all that—swimming thousands of miles to find one's way home.

Here, too, everything returns. The diamondback terrapins in their slow reassertions. The horseshoe crabs that lay their eggs in the shallows near the bulkheads in May and June—male and female locked in tandem as they go—then down to the Sargasso Sea to grow into adults before they make their return trip to the area. The purple martins fly back to their elaborate birdhouses. The snakes, the shiners, snappers, mussels—all come home. The osprey too, and their spectacular air shows. Even the skunks have returned to these parts, after having been nearly killed off by the pesticide that poisoned their food. Now chlordane is banned, and the skunks come back, along with the kingfishers and the autumn olive bushes and the red cedars, and the tall reeds of the phragmites, and the snow and the cold. Again, I paddle past the fish skeleton, a backbone with the ribs picked clean. Everything returns.

———

The epic voyages of the Greeks always ended with a return home. Heroes would sail as far as the Hesperides at the western end of the Mediterranean, and then turn back toward what they felt was their proper place in the world. So too for the Jews, whose communal story consists of continuous departure, return, and renewal. Exodus became the rise of David and the reclaiming of Canaan as promised to Abraham and Jacob.

But in the New World, epic voyages did not tend toward a return. They went relentlessly forward. Their objectives were perpetual exploration and conquest, Columbus, Cartier, and Verrazano moving in one direction only, like everything in the New World since. The Greeks and Jews had a more satisfying sense of adventure, I think. Every voyage brought them home, even if the home to which they returned was not the one they left.

⎯⎯

No such prohibition applies to the father of the bride. So I got a look at you as you stood in your room before the full-length mirror on the closet door. The short sleeves, the long train. White, like a doll's dress. And there, as I stood admiring, all the years returned—of new sneakers and new jeans and volleyball games and birthday parties and the time (age two?) you got your head caught between the balusters of the staircase and I pried open the wooden bars with my hands, like Samson, to free you, and the teachers you liked and the teachers you didn't, and the proms and the boyfriends, and the waitressing and the cheerful survival of any mishap and the intelligence to tell a disappointment from a disaster. In the mirror you looked like another person, looking at you, looking at her.

⎯⎯

The Greeks took a fancy to stories about exiled princes, who roamed the world unknown and poorly treated until some deus ex machina plopped down and restored them to their rightful place. These are justice stories, basically. Orophernis, son of Ariarathis, was expelled from his ancestral palace in Cappadocia. When the Syrians took back Cappadocia, they made the boy king.

American justice stories usually depend on the courts. The case of Robert Kearns, for instance, who invented the intermittent windshield wiper. The Ford Motor Company stole his invention. And, after twelve years of suffering and humiliation, Kearns sued and won millions.

Most justice stories are like those of Orophernis and Kearns. An unscrupulous, powerful person or institution commits a gross wrong against an innocent, who eventually prevails. The effect of such stories depends on one's belief that the hero deserves vindication, as well as a victory against a monstrous foe.

The Winslow Boy is a justice story—about an English schoolboy accused of stealing. The Winslow family engages the most celebrated barrister in England, who takes the case solely because he believes that an injustice has been committed. Since the Royal Navy runs the school the boy attended, the case brought against the school is also brought against the government. The Winslow boy goes up against England. The family is nearly broke because of court costs and is shunned and ridiculed by their former friends. But, as we have come to expect, they win their case. The barrister has a motto on his door: "Let right be done." That's the wish we bring to justice stories—let right be done—which gives us such pleasure and satisfaction.

———

Then again, there was Frank McCourt, who died a year or so after Amy, of a melanoma on his knee. A little sore he left unattended. Melanoma. The mad dog of cancer. It shot to his brain and he was dead in three months. He wrote two gorgeous memoirs. He ennobled the life of the high school teacher. He stuck by his students. He never let you down. He was generous. He loved to sing. He would lose himself in laughter, with helpless eyes, like a little boy. He blew me a good-bye kiss from his hospice bed. A goddamn sore on his knee.

———

Carl and Wendy had baby Nate the year after Amy died. A friend suggested that the renewal of life constitutes a just response to death. Pity that death has to come first.

———

"You think that an injustice has been done, don't you?" she said.

"Don't *you*? A woman of thirty-eight. A husband without a wife. Children minus a mother. What would you call it?"

"I'm not sure I would call it an injustice. I would have to be aware of the rules before I was sure they'd been broken."

"That's just sophistry."

"Maybe," she said. "But if you go around brooding about a cosmic injustice, you're going to want to redress it."

"And I can't."

"And you can't. Is that another injustice? An injustice within an injustice?" I shrugged. "Wouldn't it be smarter to figure out what you *can* do?"

———

An additional blood test showed that I have something called Graves' disease. Figures. But the disease is simply named for an Irish doctor, Robert James Graves. It is an autoimmune disease, producing an overactive thyroid, a metabolic imbalance known as hyperthyroidism. Symptoms are anxiety, irritability, and anger. No wonder they couldn't tell I was ill. The condition is easily treated with a sequence of pills. They don't know what causes Graves'. Some say stress.

The self-absorption of people as compared to that green-head fly, for instance. It looks outside itself, driven by a single purpose—to bite me. I hate my self-absorption these days. It makes me ill, literally. *This* is graves' disease. Illness leads back to self-absorption. Out here on the creek, the greenhead fly will think only about me. When he bites, I too will think about me. I am less attractive than a greenhead fly.

⁓

Kayaking suits bad-tempered people. George Hitchcock founded a poetry magazine called *Kayak*, in 1964. Its statement of purpose was printed with every issue: "A kayak is not a galleon, ark, coracle or speedboat. It is a small, water-tight vessel operated by a single oarsman. It is submersible, has sharply-pointed ends, and is constructed of light poles and the skins of furry animals. It has never yet been successfully employed as a means of mass transport." Hitchcock himself had sharply pointed ends, and edges. His dismissive rejection slips abjured the traditional savage politeness of the genre and included Victorian engravings of beheadings and mountain climbers in free fall, accompanied by take-a-hike captions. In his long, belligerent lifetime, he tried to unionize dairy farmers in California. Summoned by the House

Un-American Activities Committee in 1957, he declared his profession to be gardening. "I do underground work on plants." Famously cheap, he printed an issue of *Kayak* on paper rejected by the army for target practice. He ceased the publication of *Kayak* after sixty-four issues. "Any more, and it would risk seeming an institution," he said.

⁓

Kayak. Ducky word. You can kick it. Hack it. Whack it. You can knock it over. In Kansas, Kashmir, or Karachi. It comes back OK, like cork. K-A-Y-A-K. And me, lucky kid, propped half cocked in the cockpit pocket of my palindrome.

I am a fan of nouns. I tell my writing students that if they need three modifiers to describe something, they've probably chosen the wrong something. The noun carries its own weight, and the right one will not be made prettier or tastier or more important by anything that decorates it. It has all it needs. It contains what Emerson called "the speaking language of things." The noun. The heron. The tide. The creek. The kayak.

⁓

Jane Freeman has written a clever piece she calls "A Fish Tale," in which she weaves together, in a story, some 330 nautical terms in common usage—shove off, long shot, hell's bells, true colors, first-rate, bigwig, fluke, loggerheads, hunky-dory, feeling blue, and on and on. So many references. A loose cannon. A drifter. Sea legs. The English language, it seems, is water based. Other languages too, I guess. The world talks to itself from the sea, ship to shore. I recently learned that "rival" comes from rivers, or streams, meaning someone on the opposite side of the same stream. And that the devil in "the devil and the deep blue sea" does not refer to Satan, but rather to the line on the hull where the water meets the vessel. To be caught between the devil and the deep blue sea does not mean you have a choice. It means you're a goner.

And there's the verb "to fret." A river can fret away at its banks, and that which is fretted is corroded. Something that eats away at us may be said to fret the mind or the heart. We use the word to denote a form of worry or vexation. The phrase "don't fret" is gentler than the image of a heart or a mind being abraded, or filed down like a riverbank.

———

But I shall follow the endless, winding way,—
the flowing river in the cave of man.
—HERMAN MELVILLE, *PIERRE*

———

Once I looked around me, I saw that I had taken the wrong exit. It was a Sunday in April, on my drive back to Quogue. I took the wrong exit off the Southern State, a highway I have driven twice a week for over two years. I probably could do it blindfolded. Yet I drifted into a mistake and found myself driving past a row of modern town houses on a street in West Islip. The houses were brick and uniform, celibate but pleasant. Everyone has to live somewhere. People who make their lives in West Islip are content to call those houses home.

Having a general sense of where I was, I knew that I easily could find my way back to the Southern State, but I dawdled awhile. I drove slowly and wondered what it would be like to live in West Islip. If I knocked at a door, would a family welcome me in? I might ask them if they knew of a town house available for rent or sale. I might move in and buy furniture. I might apply for a teaching job at the local high school, where I might make a friend or two on the faculty, and we could have lunch now and then. I might join the Elks Club or the Kiwanis.

Since it was the beginning of spring, I might volunteer to coach Little League in town. And there would be other things I might do, like head the blood drive or help out in the library. Before I drove away, I thought how good it might feel to watch the tulips and the geese return to the area after the long winter, and to smell the thawed earth as I paced up and down in the coach's box off first, cheering on my kids, at a Little League game in West Islip.

———

Elizabeth Bishop said, "The art of losing isn't hard to master." The point is, one needs practice.

———

Whenever scientists talk about communication among sea creatures, they bring up whales and dolphins, tuna once in a while. The beasts of the sea. All the big fish. Do the little ones under my kayak chat with one another as well? The great animals communicate like cellos. If the shiners communicate, I bet they babble like chatterboxes. Such a commotion. Why stop at fish? What are the insects gossiping about? What code are the woodpeckers tapping in? How brayeth the gulls? It's just a guess. No one has heard them. No one has bothered to listen. What if dolphins have nothing to say but blather, and the lower orders are yammering game theory?

The sky's grayness is diffuse, as it is in concrete or in stone. On such a morning, I imagine, pioneers rolled west in clunky wagons, or Edison tested his incandescent lightbulb, or Yeats looked up and dreamed a swan. The past looks like this. Gray. I clamber down a ladder and peer in, but all I see is a leprous light with cardboard figures in the wrong places. Memory is sluggish, like a donkey in the briar. It is born to fail.

At any rate, something may be redeemed in the attempt— to get back one clear picture before night falls. The paddle dips to its own rhythm. It buries itself in the welcoming water. I look up like a puppy, eager for a sign.

Some night, I should like to try stargazing. Get hold of a collapsible, portable Maksutov telescope and set it up behind the house or, better, here on the banks of the creek. I'd need a basic star chart and a flashlight to read it by, but nothing more. The advantage of being an amateur in most things, including kayaking, is that all any enterprise requires is love. Love hides in the word *amateur*. I would park myself, set up my scope, and wait till my eyes were accustomed to the dark. It's what we do in any investigation. The mind is an eye in the socket of the past. And the stars are past. I read somewhere that when the universe runs out of time, it fades to total darkness, like life itself. I should like to see as far as that.

———

A rerun of the movie *Ghost* was on TV recently. It was always my favorite of the talk-with-the-dead films because of the unflagging effort of the murdered man, Patrick Swayze, to get back to his beloved, Demi Moore. When he attempts to touch her, his hand goes through her body, or her body goes through his hand. But he tries and tries again, pawing the air like a bear, until at last his hand feels something. Am I remembering this accurately? I didn't watch the rerun of *Ghost*, and I do not recall how Swayze does it. But I'm pretty sure that's the way he saves the woman he loves from danger. His will is so strong, he makes air tangible. Does Swayze try to touch the living now?

———

"How do you make a ghost?" one of the kids' friends asked me on the afternoon before last Halloween. Later, he appeared with the sheet on cockeyed and his head stuck in the sleeve. "Can you fix this?" he asked me. I told him yes. I could fix that.

In Bethesda the other night, the children were chasing fireflies. One of those hot, strawberry-jam nights of a Maryland summer, when thought is driven from the mind. Ginny, Harris, and I watched the children bolt from quarry to quarry, holding empty jelly bottles with holes poked in the caps. They ran up and down the driveway and the lawn in front of the house. "I've got one! No, he escaped!" Harris was sitting on the hood of Ginny's car. I was sitting on the front steps. Ginny was standing near James, anxious that he might fall. We proceeded into the dark, watching for the brief explosions of light. Ginny said, "Isn't this a miracle."

The first time we drove down to Bethesda, and we came to the Harbor Tunnel in Baltimore, there was a road sign: "No Hazmats." We called you. "What's a Hazmat?" we asked.

Not in terror but in stillness will the world come to an end. (Without even a whimper.) One feels the end imminently.

Something about the casual jubilation in response to un-important things, and the nature of events—the bulletins about low mortgage rates and the eager self-exposures on Facebook. It takes more than that to sink a ship, I know. And I realize that it's wrong to read the universe in one's mood. But hell. I have run away from my regiment without earning my red badge, and there isn't a hell of a lot to do these days but go kayaking and project. Speaking of my reg-iment, have you noticed how many novels are written about the First World War, like *Regeneration?* They seem lovesick pursuits of an earlier Armageddon when noise was involved. The Great War was purposeless, of course. Knuckles and knee joints flying every which way. But at least you could hear the destruction. Now we have the stillness of brood-ing madmen all over the world, drumming their fingers on tables of air. No screams. No chop of boats. Cal Lowell sits like Stonehenge at the head of the seminar table, contem-plating sending Czar Lepke a file with a chocolate layer cake inside. *My* mind's not right.

I should reread that part of *Specimen Days* in which nurse Walt Whitman is attending the Union fallen and near dead in the U.S. Patent Office in Washington, D.C., which doubled as a hospital during the Civil War—where he notes, with hardly a trace of irony, that the same species capable of coming up with the most dazzling inventions made of wood and brass was just as capable of blowing off one another's limbs. The hall was filled with bright machines side by side with men on cots, massaging their new stumps.

In Moscow, September 1987, a professor at the university and I took a walk in the city at a celebration of the seventieth anniversary of the Russian Revolution.

"The people notice you," she said. "Can you tell?"

"Yes, but why? Do I look so different from everyday Russians?"

"You don't look afraid."

Prosaic nightmares visit me in my half sleep. The wrong presentation when I am teaching. An altercation with the cable man or the cleaners. The nightmares of the middle class, of Russian civil servants under the czar. I enter a great hall packed with hundreds of people sitting at school desks and experience the tepid fear of writing an exam for a course I never took. They ought to be classier, these nightmares, scarier. They ought to involve recriminations, old shames and sins, reconfigured into symbols. I should be running away from the sheriff's bloodhounds, thrashing through thickets and breathing hard, weighed down by the chains of my chain gang. Instead, I am walking along and I come across a little pool of water rotting a hole in a tree, or an aphid gnawing on a leaf. A doctor takes my pulse and pronounces me alive. Small craft advisories. The passionless heart goes everywhere, even to sleep. What will I dream tonight?

———

On the wide beach in Latvia, my guide pointed out a man who was trudging in the sand with his head bowed. He said the man had fallen into a state of neglect ever since his daughter died. Neglect, as when a town in which an industry once thrived (a steel mill or a shoe factory) is fallen from neglect, and the eaves of the roofs sag, soaked with rain, and the doors of the bank vault lie open to houseflies, and the grocer's shelves are thick with dust, and the druggist's shelves the same. And nothing remains of the schoolyard but a jungle gym in a heap of pipes and a chain-link fence that has been yanked from its stanchions. My guide said that's what happens when you let yourself go. I don't know. It might have been neglect. It seemed more willful than neglect.

—

Daughter. Water. I turn my boat. The point I am approaching was bought about one hundred fifty years ago by the Penniman family, who bought it from the Herrick family, who had bought it from the Hallocks. The earliest Herrick had two sons, who had fought in the Revolutionary War— one a patriot, one a Tory. I know nothing of George Penniman, who named my creek, and very little of Quogue history, except the date of the founding of the village, 1659. There are worthy folks around here who spend chunks of their lives studying local history. Andrew Botsford, associate editor of the *Southampton Press*, was born here. It tickles me to rile him by saying something like "I was in Quiogue [the neighboring village] the other day, Andrew." He steams, "You do not say 'in Quiogue,' as I have told you a thousand times. Quiogue is an island. You say, 'on Quiogue.'" I tell him I'll remember that the next time I'm in Quiogue.

Dick Gardner, one of Quogue's historians, sent me a pastel watercolor postcard of Penniman's Creek done in the 1880s. It shows the place where I enter and exit the creek, though there is no ramp in the picture, and there are no grand houses. The trees are cut down, for livestock and farming. The creek looks flat and shiny, lying in a dead calm. Beyond it, a strip of ocean is visible, as it is today. Above it, a pale pink sky fades to light blue. The watercolor is called *Anchorage*, for several white sailboats anchored in the creek.

I have tried to pay attention to Quogue history, but little of it interests me. Books and pamphlets tell of the slaves that were kept here, and of the importance of Quogue Street, on which we live, to seventeenth- and eighteenth-century traffic, and of the Hurricane of 1938, when the Atlantic rose eighteen feet, that killed three people, drowned several houses, and tossed boats on the lawns. I am taken more by the thought of the shipwrecks, and of whales that were hunted in the ocean, and in the inlets too, like Penniman's Creek, until they were killed off. Smears of blood on the water. The great beasts gasping for air. What would I do if my kayak were hoisted upon the head of a sudden whale, directly over the blowhole? "I thought you were dead," I'd tell the whale, who would reply, "I thought the same of you."

———

A friend was surprised one night when I remarked that I have never envied anyone. I did not mean that as a point of pride. Envy corrupts innocence—the innocence of the one who feels envy and that of its object. Enough has been said of the dead, but I am certain they do not feel envy, least of all of the living. They may feel longing, which is different.

Oh, what the hell. Isn't everything dead? Nations are made up of the dead. Myths extol the dead. Laws and policies, dead. The old lies, dead as doornails. The doornails, dead, and the screws and the boards and the bricks. Sentiments dead. The statues of the dead in the parks. The anthems and parades, and the wars and the war dead, dead. The dead are in the old movies and in the old songs, in the books, on the plaques, and in the portraits in the galleries, which too are dead. The names on the street signs, the names of the living, all dead. We stomp about in gardens of ashes.

What do you say, Big Man—are you up for a trade? One of those cloak-and-dagger swaps they used to make at the Berlin Wall, one double agent for another? Suppose I told you that I possessed valuable information, including dates and photographs and maps on microfilm. Are you game? Tell you what. I'll wait in the back of the car, hidden from the soldiers patrolling the gates, till you decide.

NO WAKE

—A SIGN AT THE MOUTH OF THE CANAL

⌒

Hope. Hope. Where is thy market now? And. And. And, take Odysseus, please. The man had everything—danger, fame, any woman any time. And he was a bona fide hero. And he had wiles and wit. Yet every one of his adventures ends in a loss of one sort or another. And when he finally sails into port, there is no one to love him but the wife he left and the son he does not recognize. This is the myth we preserve above all others, involving a perilous voyage and defeat. It seems to be what we wish to assure ourselves of—that the life of the best of the lot, the strongest and bravest and smartest, is without hope. "Be kind, for everyone you meet is carrying a great burden."

⌒

They do not eat pig.
They do not expose their faces.
They say, "Did I do that?"
They say, "The first known bird is the archaeopteryx."
They are tired.
They are deadly. They run over children, and drive on.

They dance in public places.

They toss a perfect spiral.

They speak of money, great amounts of money.

They speak of colors. They speak of flutes.

They are Haitian. No, Malaysian.

They marry their own.

They marry others.

They are admirers of yours.

They have lost limbs, sawed off at the elbow joints and knees.

They have just bought the iPhone. And will you look at this? And will you look at this?

They teach, they yearn, they come, they go.

My father decided to wait till we were in the car and he was driving me to school before he told me that Miss Jourdan had died. I was six. No one I knew had ever died, but the finality in his voice told me what death meant. I asked no questions. She had been the most forceful and imposing of the three ladies who lived together in the apartment above ours at 36 Gramercy Park. They lived on the tenth floor, we on the ninth. Since the age of four, I had been going up to visit the ladies in the afternoons, when my mother was still working at her school. They would read to me—*Tom Sawyer, Doctor Dolittle,* and *The Wind in the Willows.* They taught me canasta, at which they openly cheated.

Miss Prescott was a librarian at Columbia, Miss Cutler a watercolorist and ceramicist. Miss Jourdan was a novelist and was also the editor of *Harper's Bazaar* magazine. The two others deferred to her. The ladies' apartment was dark wood, with crossed swords and shields bearing coats of arms on the walls and maroon velvet on the window seats. A suit of armor stood in the middle of the entrance hall. There was a wastepaper basket made from the foot of a rhinoceros, and a little elephant carved from ivory. As a child, I saw it as noteworthy that someone would carve an elephant out of ivory, but I made no comment.

Toward the end of the afternoons, Miss Jourdan would return from work. She greeted her companions tersely, laid down her briefcase, and looked me over. She was a large woman, who breathed heavily and always dressed in black, like Queen Victoria. Rarely would she join the canasta games, but rather would go straight to the concert grand in the living room and play, her huge hands extending nearly two octaves and coming down hard on the keys.

One day she played "The Blue Danube" and "London-

derry Aire." I listened. And when she was finished, I sat beside her on the piano bench and played the two pieces pretty
much as she had done, though with simpler chords and a
lighter touch. Miss Cutler and Miss Prescott shrieked with
excitement at my small accomplishment. Miss Jourdan simply gave me an abrupt nod of approval.

Thirty-six Gramercy Park was constructed of white
terra-cotta, stood twelve stories high, and was shaped like
a square U. Outside, two white stone knights on pedestals
flanked a long green awning. Near the top of the building
were stone gargoyles that stuck out into the open space. The
moving men had to be careful as they worked their ropes
and pulleys around the gargoyles when, a year after Miss
Jourdan died, they hoisted our new piano through the living
room window. Home from school, I stood in front of the awning looking up and watching the great black harp-shaped
case rise nine stories into the sky.

Most impressive, mister, I'm sure. But tell me: if your ear is
so great, why did it not pick up the strangler's footsteps near
her heart?

The place I'll wind up at the end of my life, I inform my friends, who are uninterested, is the grubbiest bar in Hampton Bays, the semitough town situated between Quogue and Southampton. There I'll spend most of my remaining days and all of my nights sitting in a dark corner—my teeth yellowed, my face unshaven—drinking Thunderbird, when I can get it. Students from Stony Brook will come in, point me out to a newcomer, and snigger, "Why don't you buy that old bird a Jameson's? He'll tell you about all the U.S. presidents he's met!" Then they'll laugh.

Ford was the nicest. Nixon the most unnerving. I was about to interview Nixon for a story in 1985 on the fortieth anniversary of Hiroshima. When I placed my tape recorder in front of him, he said, "Oh. That's a new tape recorder. They're so much *better* than the old tape recorders." I met with Carter on a day that he seemed pissed off about something, but he was cordial. I met with Clinton several times, even watched a basketball game with him. I flew in Air Force One with George Bush, the daddy. Of them all, I most liked Reagan, for his personality, not his politics. I did the 1980 "Man of the Year" story on him for *Time*.

He was also involved in a *Time* essay I did two years later, called "The Man in the Water." It was about the Air

Florida crash in the Potomac River in 1982, and specifically about the man who stood in the freezing water and who died serving as a human lifeline to the other passengers. Reagan read from the piece in a speech honoring the man's courage and nobility. Funny to recall it now, "The Man in the Water."

In a kayak, the correct position for your legs is to bend them slightly as they extend to the foot pegs. You paddle with your arms bent as well, and you work the paddle by pushing your hands out toward the blades as you rotate your arms. Feels awkward, but you get used to it.

It is after ten. I read the sun. The water looks like melting asphalt, the way asphalt looks at high noon in August, when you can see the ripples. There's a sailboat, a little Sunfish. It's the first moving vessel other than my own I have seen this morning. I resent sharing the water with it, even if it is gliding away from me in the canal outside my creek. I glower. When the kids were small, we had a farmhouse in Canaan, New Hampshire. The town was founded by a man named Schofield, who moved his family north from Connecticut in the mid-1700s. He built his house in the woods in the dead of winter. Come spring, he heard a single gunshot and moved his family to Canada, because Canaan was getting too crowded.

———

Change? She meant a sea change. She meant my soul. How do I change my soul? What change do you require, Amy? Name it.

———

The news reports that a tribute Mark Twain wrote after his daughter's death has been auctioned for $245,000. The tribute runs sixty-four pages and has not been published. I should like to see it. I read something of Twain's after the death of his younger brother, Henry, who was working on a riverboat when it caught fire and exploded. Before Henry died of burns, Twain went to visit him. He wrote the Clemens family a letter out of his shattered heart: "Long before this reaches you, my poor Henry—my darling, my pride, my glory, my *all*, will have finished his blameless career, and the light of my life will have gone out in utter darkness."

Fire and water. When the proverbial problem was put to Camus—if your house was on fire, what would you take from it for safekeeping?—he said, "The fire." If your house was flooded, would you take the water? It is one thing to talk of embracing fire or water, quite another to do it.

⁓

Death by water. The Japanese ceremony of Obon involves the floating of illuminated lanterns in rivers, lakes, and seas, to guide the dead spirits back into their world. In Ancient Egypt, the funerary boat that carried Cheops's body to Giza was 143 feet long and 19½ feet wide, said to have a displacement of 45 tons. Other boats were smaller. The British Museum displays a model twelfth-century wooden funerary boat bearing a mummy on a bier beneath a canopy. To the port side stands the figure of a priest. Fore and aft of the mummy are two women mourners, archetypal representations of Isis and Nephthys. The boat is driven by a helmsman who sits alone between a pair of oars.

Is drowning easier? The movies show James Mason walking into the Pacific. Faulkner has Quentin sidling into the Charles River. Virginia Woolf stuffed her pockets with rocks and stepped into the Thames. *The Perfect Storm* sets things straight about drowning—water entering the lungs, changing the blood chemistry, causing the blood to become more concentrated. The heart cannot bear the extra weight. Sebastian Junger's description of drowning probably turned all those who were considering it to thoughts of shotguns. Why did people ever think that death by water was peaceful? Yearning for the original home? I dip my hand over the side and feel the cold. My skin jumps.

———

How many sailors drown at sea without anyone knowing they went under? So their loved ones—wives, sweethearts, mothers—continue praying for their safe return. The sun sinks, the sun rises optimistically. On the widow's walk someone with a spyglass looks out on the shelves of the ocean, searching for a sail or a waving, desperate hand. She has worn a new dress in case this is the day. The drowned sailor may know what his beloved is going through, her endless looking, but he is unable to send a telegram regretting to inform her of his passing. He lies on his bed of plankton, green fleece, and pearls in a forest of kelp. He thinks, how beautiful it is here. I wish Mary could see it. At that moment, Mary is called inside. Something inconsequential has diverted her attention from her vigil. When she returns to her post, she wonders if she has missed a sail or a hand.

———

Any minute now, my ship is coming in.
I'll keep checking the horizon . . .
—SONG HEARD IN HERTZ RENT-A-CAR AD ON TV

⌣

Americans do not believe in death, which is why we are forever shocked by its intrusions. Democracy and socialism, both fantasies, are undergirded by the idea that death happens to other people. When the latest Bush administration forbade television reporters from photographing the coffins of American soldiers, it was a way of affirming that death does not exist here and is merely a rumor. Even our cemeteries seem like anomalies on the landscape.

In Japan, after a flash flood, the cemeteries built on the hillsides become waterlogged. Coffins rise and float out of the earth and ride into the villages, fishtailing on the liquid streets and banging on the doors of the houses.

⌣

"Let's talk of graves, of worms, and epitaphs," said Richard II, contemplating his final deposition. Let's do. Such spirited communities, cemeteries. Assisted dying facilities. Novodevichy Cemetery in Moscow, where even today thousands bring flowers to lay at the graves of Gogol and Chekhov.

Green-Wood Cemetery in Brooklyn. Boss Tweed is buried there, along with Currier and Ives, Charles Tiffany the jeweler, Pierre Lorillard the tobacco tycoon, and Frank Morgan, the Wizard of Oz. Closer to here, Jack Dempsey and Gary Cooper are buried in cemeteries in Southampton. Tour guides point out their graves. One never knows how to react to celebrities in a cemetery.

I wonder what it's like to work in such places—do the digging and the patting down. Those workers accomplish the impossible and live with the dead. Do they feel closer to their charges? Or are they more aware of the distance between them? Are gravediggers unionized? Are they paid by the hole? I never catch sight of them, but they could be hanging around in the shade, propped up against the side of a mausoleum, nursing a beer, and peering through slits of eyes at the people who come to the cemeteries bearing living flowers for Gogol, Chekhov, and others.

One night in Sudan, the boys gathered in a circle, aiming their flashlights at the ground, as if to create a campfire, and told stories. Their favorite was about a man named Hornbill who disregarded the customs of his village and refused even to attend services for the dead. When Hornbill's own child

died, the other villagers refused to tell him where the graveyard was located. "Where are the graves?" Hornbill asked
everyone he passed on the road, as he carried his child on his
back. But no one would tell him where the graveyard was.
So he walked the earth forever, his dead child on his back,
crying, "Where are the graves?"

———

What is the routine in winter? I wonder. I haven't been
there then but twice. The first time was in December, which
was the first time for you as well. The second, on the first
anniversary. Since then I have gone only in the warmer
months. I don't know why. The facts do not change accord-
ing to the seasons. Do the squirrels form a cortege to amuse
themselves? Do the birds, their prairies extending forever,
complain about the paucity of seeds? The deer, the paucity
of flowers? My heart patrols the graves of others as I check
out your neighborhood. Ice padlocks the sepulchers. The
frozen earth as numb as stone. You lie beneath the obscene
folds of snow.

———

And therefore I have paddled my kayak on the creek and
come to the holy village of Quogue. Ginny tells me that I

sigh a lot. I was not aware of it. I don't know what it means. To sigh. To exhale a long, deep breath to signify a response to good news or bad news. To indicate passion, as in "a sigh is just a sigh." To express weariness or relief. A sigh comes at the end of a loud laugh, too. I doubt that Ginny is thinking of relief, weariness, passion, or laughter. The sound one makes when he hasn't enough air. The sound one makes before drowning. The sound of surrender, perhaps.

Waterloo. The Battle of Waterloo (June 18, 1815) ended Napoleon's spectacular military career, as well as twenty-three years of recurrent conflict between France and the rest of Europe. The word first appeared in casual use the following year, 1816, meaning a decisive or final setback or defeat.

At the top of the bookshelf, *The Enneads* by Plotinus was leaning like a drunk against the wall. I took it down and opened it by chance to the section on beauty. I have the book because I did my PhD dissertation on Stephen MacKenna, an Irish journalist in the late nineteenth century, whose life-work was to translate Plotinus. I'd gone to Ireland intending to do my thesis on Synge, but in a bookstore in Dublin I came upon *The Journal and Letters of Stephen MacKenna* by E. R. Dodds, Regius Professor of Classics at Oxford. I wrote to Dodds. He invited me to his Oxford cottage. He poured me two stiff gins and gave me all the MacKenna papers in his possession, on the proviso that I give them to the Irish National Library when I was done with them.

What appealed to me about MacKenna was the quality of his thought—not profound, but generous. He led a simple life, which I admired—free of possessions, free to reflect on the worthiness of life and to be as noble as the heart allows. He was a friend to wilder men, Synge and Joyce, who could write rings around MacKenna. But they recognized the plain goodness of a modest man who knew how to live. Be kind, for everyone you meet is carrying a great burden.

A rich man is honored more than a talented one because money is something people understand. The house towering before me at the narrow end of the creek is, I assume, a rich man's house. Everything about it is startling and unambiguous. Its level lawn. Its boathouse shaped like a lighthouse, with filigree where the lamp would be. Its great heavy door, its four chimneys, its many bedrooms and bathrooms, and its country kitchen to die for, with a picture window facing me. I used to covet such a place. Now I look at it as if it were a Pueblo apartment or an igloo, and I on a tour of the American Museum of Natural History, peering into the strange living quarters of waxy distant peoples. The big house means nothing. Its loud success discourages me. All I want of a home is what I have—room for family, room for work. In Bethesda, Ginny and I live in one room with a bath connected. I can write there when the kids are in school. When they're home, they're welcome to pile in. Kids like tight places, where everyone is squeezed together.

At home in Quogue, the glass door in the kitchen is smudged with palm prints and kiss marks and streaks made by small fingers. The glass in the picture window of the house before me is stain-free and sanitized. I keep my glass door as it is. I avoid Lysol. I eschew Windex.

———

While in this corner, a crow with the head of a gambler addresses a waterlogged tree trunk and takes a peck. He's in charge, and he knows it. After a night of whoring, booze, and Texas Hold 'Em, he is ready for the new day of dissipation. No crisis of conscience disturbs his plans. He harbors no guilt, no remorse. Never humbled, he does not eat . . . he chuckles at the thought. He asks himself no philosophical question—is there life after crows? He has no politics. He does not vote. His education is limited. He has read neither John Dryden nor Edmund Spenser, not even John Ransom. ("Why, son, Crowe is mah middle name!") He yearns for nothing he cannot have. Prince of Halloween, he is impervious to insults. Unloved, unadmired, inelegant (that voice!). He could not care less. Born a crow, die a crow. A crow in every feature. He surveys the world that was designed for crows—telephone wires, jungle gyms, meadows of flowers, harvests, roadkill—all created with crows in mind. He licks no wounds. He misses no one. The black sheen of his morning coat fits him like a glove.

Is this France, Albuquerque, or Greece? I paddle to the mouth of the creek and stare eagerly toward the canal, and beyond. A few strokes and I am in Portugal. A few more, China. Where is my spirit of adventure? Time was, I would go anywhere, especially alone. I would go anywhere alone. My eyes burned. I could see into the dark. The tip of my kayak touches the crosscurrents. The sun flecks the water like salmon skins. All it would take is a stretch of the forearms. Yet I paddle backward into the creek.

Now I move to the far side.

Now I sing, "Show me the way to go home."

Now I loaf with my paddle athwart the gunwales.

Now I recall soft-boiled eggs in an egg-shaped dish.

Now I acknowledge the breeze on my knuckles.

Now I paddle again. The kayak surges on.

Now I dream the kids are little, and I am coming through the door.

As to that, I see a light in the ground-floor window of the last house on the promontory. We are there in that room, gathered at the breakfast table, passing round the warm bread. Look out the window. See? There. A man in a kayak, alone in the creek. He looks familiar. Do you know him?

⸻

We hitched a mattress to the roof of the car and plowed north from Cambridge to our farmhouse. March in New Hampshire. The gas froze in the tank. Of course, when we got to the house, crunching the hard snow in the driveway, the heat was out. That winter it was out more than on. We stuck you and Carl in your beds and made a mound of blankets. I draped myself on top of the blankets and stayed till you were asleep.

You hated the cold. You'd plant yourself like a little

statue, fold your arms in passive resistance, and cry. There was more to it than that. Teaching where I did not want to be. Work I didn't want to do. Mired in respectability. We all were out of place. I think you sensed it, two-and-a-half-year-old you, in your pint-size misery and your pink snowsuit. I think you sensed everything, including your different heart.

A bird lay dead at the door of the barn, stuck to the snow. "Does everything die?" you asked. I picked it up and tossed it in the woods. It left a stain. How easily parents sweep their children in their arms. How snug they feel. That night, the house at 40 degrees, you were warm at last beneath the doll blankets and the navy surplus blankets and the Goodwill duvet, and me.

⁓

Dead ahead: directly ahead.

Dead astern: directly behind.

Dead reckoning: calculating distance by using time on the water and estimated paddling speed.

⁓

And by using the wind. On the water, wind is everything. In 1805, Sir Francis Beaufort devised his scale of wind speed. It proved indispensable to the British navy, which used the wind as its fuel source. Even in this little creek, wind speed is important. The wind makes waves, and I cannot hit wave after wave without fatiguing myself. If I proceed to shore and go straight in, I'll be caught in the trough of the waves. So I have to angle across the water and use the wind to my advantage.

In 1984, four thousand residents of Bhopal, India, were killed by a toxic gas leak. After the gas dissipated, officials examined the affected area. It turned out that some people were living normally, as they always had, while adjacent streets were strewn with bodies. Everything depended on where the wind was blowing.

⸻

I was fifty-three before I saw my first dead person, in Sudan, in a camp called Palotaka. He was an eleven-year-old named Thon, who had died of diarrhea and dehydration, like many of the boys on their trek from Khartoum. Others were killed by animals or drowned in the swollen rivers. Thon was wrapped in a white cotton cloth. I held him in my arms. Light as a sheet of paper. The breath went out of him like a drop from a vial.

The next time I saw a dead person—many dead people— was in Rwanda, where I was writing a piece for the *New York*

Times Magazine. I stood on a yellow bridge over the Kagera River and watched the macheted bodies rise and topple over a waterfall. One, thirty, a hundred. They fell and spun in eddies, or got caught in pools, or were carried out to Lake Victoria. Their skin seemed bleached. They tumbled like pieces of chalk.

The third time was my mother. Even in death, her face was anxious. My father died while I was out of the country, of congestive heart failure. He attempted to treat it himself. The dead person I saw most recently was you.

———

Some say we idealize the dead—their sublime looks, their punch lines and wise remarks. You do not want me to do that, I know. You were always too honest. Only, honestly, I never noticed a flaw. And if I saw one emerge when you were little, and I mentioned it, you would correct it so deftly that the correction became a superseding virtue.

"Oh, come on, Dad. I was just an ordinary girl who made ordinary mistakes. You'll only screw things up for both of us if you paint me as a goddess. I never wanted to be perfect. And you yourself used to warn us about believing in perfect things. Besides, you're regressing. Shouldn't you be getting somewhere?"

"You, too?"

"Define your problem, understand it, and try to solve it. That was *your* advice."

"Sorry, Amy. I cannot hear you. I can't communicate with the dead. Remember?"

———

Sammy was playing with a handheld game that claims to be able to name anything you're thinking of. It is very clever and even taunts the players before giving the answer—"Is that the best you can do?" Sammy thought of "typewriter," and eventually the nasty little computer figured it out, by asking increasingly delimiting questions. The answers you can give are "Yes," "No," or "Sometimes." Sammy came up with "heaven." The computer was stumped. It asked, "Does it make you happy?" Sammy pushed: "Sometimes."

I like to imagine a different sort of heaven, without pudgy angels, white pillars, and that dreadful music. What I imagine is not a place but a feeling—one ripple of a moment where everything is accepted, for a change. If that were heaven, you could enjoy it, say, at breakfast, when you've sipped your orange juice and your coffee and are about to sink your teeth into a slice of buttered toast.

———

"Another day in paradise," said the girl with the bright blue eyes as she passed me in Southampton the other morning—instead of saying, "Will you cloak me in your arms and shield me from the killing sun?"

"Another day in paradise," I answered her—instead of saying, "Yes. Of course. And from the rain. And from the sleet."

———

Water is groundless. It has no basis, like art. It is the answer to no one's question. I love the feel of it. Paddling, I churn up great bulbous drops, splash my arms, my legs, my face. The taste of salt. I lick my lips. Drenched. Soaked to the bone, as if I had just risen from the bottom of the ocean with a trident in my hand and seaweed in my Hellenistic hair. Bathed. Cleansed. Flooded. I could live this way, forever damp as a sail, a seal, a hull, a sluice. Diluted as a column of water. My thoughts are slippery when wet.

———

The first time I swam was in Long Island Sound. I was four. My father was not with me. Yet he had taught me to swim.

Day after day at Compo Beach in Westport, Connecticut, he had stood waist-high in the low-tide kiddy ocean, holding me about the middle like a magician proving there was no possible way his assistant could be supported, only relaxing his grip by the slightest degrees as he waited for the moment I would flip off like a tadpole on my own. As long as he was there that moment never came. Feeling his support diminish, I would mount an inversely proportional panic, and by the time I was free I was lost.

But when he was away in New York one day, I swam, and I immediately hollered to my mother to see what I could do. He would have liked to see me take my first swim, I know, and I also know that I never could have swum with him close by, and worse, that I probably unconsciously timed my big moment to disappoint him or to show him up—to confound his pride and love. Some eight years later, when we were on a short family holiday on Cape Cod, he and I agreed to swim out to a float. At thirteen, I had so much strength. I never thought about it. My father kept up, his dignified crawl beside my splashy riot. But when we reached the float, his chest was heaving with dry sobs. He rested on the float a while like a beached fish before very cautiously dog-paddling back, holding on to the rope that led from the shore to the float, and sometimes holding on to me. Mortality, he explained—the last thing I wanted to hear.

After I had had children of my own, and my father and I had worked out our SALT XXXV and would meet in the summers, as world powers meet, to discuss this and that— then we were friends. At night, with everyone else asleep, we would sit together in the kitchen of some Long Island country house he had rented, talking about the past and fu- ture, even talking politics, which took a long time to learn to do without explosions, and hearing the Atlantic in the long pauses. When we were ready to turn in, I would put away the glasses, but it was always he who locked the doors. When he died, and I realized that from then on it would be up to me to lock the doors, I wanted to say: Look, Dad, it was *you* who taught me to swim.

My sons are men. As their father, I should be able to re- lieve their hurt. If I cannot get Amy back, what can I give them instead? They were conspirators, our three children— conspirators from the Latin: They breathed together. They conspired in their tastes, in their jokes, in their friends. When they needed to, they conspired against Ginny and me. Today, whenever Carl and John are together, just the two of them, they move about as if Amy were standing between them. Memory's laughter dies into sighs. Where is the third who walked beside them? A cry of absence. A cry of silence.

———

Before you know it, summer. And before you know it, the kids are dressing up in floppy Luigi hats on Halloween, before you know it. Time bounces on, gay as reggae, its stiff gaze comic, scary. Out here, no one hears my weakness. Before you know it, winter kills the sedge. Just like that.

———

Ginny sees Amy's spirit in cardinals. When the bird flies into view, she smiles. Jessie, Sammy, and James know this about her. They will call out, "Mimi! There's a cardinal!" Death in a billion cardinals. Death in thrushes, tulips, breezes. The commemorative days. All Saints. All Souls. On the Celtic holiday of Samhain, the wall between the living and the dead is said to be permeable. I'll believe it when I touch it.

Are the dead an evolving species? Is my daughter one thing in death today, another tomorrow? The wall stays up, and all you have is the dead hanging back in their adamant obscurity. I am not interested in death's properties. I don't care. The books on the subject delve like gravediggers into the symbolism of caskets and the metaphor of embalming. Death studies. They do not tell me how to live in the world without my daughter. That's my problem, Doctor.

———

If Darwin could believe in God's magnanimity, anyone can do it. He didn't indicate such a belief in the early editions of *On the Origin of Species*, but he ended the third edition with a hymn to God's praise. He wrote of the grandeur of life, "having originally been breathed by the Creator into a few forms or into one," and marveled in the thought that "from so simple a beginning endless forms most beautiful and most wonderful have been, and are being evolved." Many of his nineteenth-century challengers were surprised by his attribution of the species to a Creator. They might have been less so had they known that the one book he brought with him on his voyages on the *Beagle* was *Paradise Lost.*

Since Darwin thought all evolution random, I assume he thought the same thing about the actions of his creator, which calls into question his designation of God as the supreme designer. It would have been more consistent with his theory of evolution had he written of God as the supreme gambler, drunk on his own power and rolling the original dice. That was the God Einstein said he could not believe in.

But Einstein was no Darwin. When Amy died, I'd have been better off not believing in God. Yet the supreme dice roller is precisely the God I believe in. The God who deserts the wreckage and doesn't care. The God of my rage.

———

Montesquieu said, "If triangles had a god, it would have three sides." But it wouldn't *take* sides.

———

The afternoon Ginny and I got the phone call, I said to God, "That's the last prayer you get from me." I regret that I had ever prayed. A prayer is either a request or a song of praise. Even the hallowed "Lord's Prayer" is simply part "give us" and part "power and the glory." I have neither request nor song these days. When I did pray, it was in the spirit of a deal I made with God: I would do as little harm as I could, and he would protect me and my own. To be sure, it was I alone who proposed the bargain. He never said, "I'm in." My friend tells me that God could not save Amy, but that he weeps for her. Call that a god?

Deliver me from staring. Deliver me from shaking my head in the barber's chair. Deliver me from night. From the air and the water. From the gauze and the shears. Deliver me from books. From gates. From headstones. Deliver me from ghosts, from brutes, from the brute in me. Deliver me from me. Deliver me from you.

———

A billboard at exit 9 on the New Jersey Turnpike quotes from the Book of Revelations: "After you die, you will meet God." I can hardly wait.

———

I prefer Zeus. Crazy Zeus. Intolerant, hasty Zeus. Even the name was cool. A god like that wasn't afraid to get down and dirty with the rest of us. Mortals were his meat. He understood us, was one of us, only bigger. Lecherous Zeus. Lascivious Zeus. Vengeful, spiteful. Patroclus got his. Achilles his. Talk of mercurial! Yet with Zeus, one would have had a fighting chance, and you could always have played on his vanity—told him how mighty he was, the mightiest, the handsomest, the great god Zeus. You'd bet he could do anything, O Magnificent Zeus, if he had a mind to.

———

Or don't. Don't weave nations into harmonies. Don't take up anybody's burdens. Show your true colors in sustaining the sorrow of the world, as the gull tips and falls in the sun. Why lift a finger? You who have made all this. You who have broken it and smashed it like the seashells on the pyre-docks. Why should you, defined only by yourself, feel compelled to go the extra mile? Do I need you? Isn't loneliness enough of a god?

———

Ooomm. Ooomm. In Suriname, the howler monkeys unburden themselves at dawn. They awaken you with the mournful siren of their howling. They awaken themselves. Before they begin their day, before they brachiate from tree to tree, before they search for clutches of berries and gorge themselves on bananas, before they hunt, fight, or mate, they howl. Before they live, they howl. Ooomm. That is their sound.

———

> We are the boat, we are the sea. I sail in you. You
> sail in me.
>
> —LORRE WYATT, "SOMOS EL BARCO"

———

One summer when I was seven, I contracted an ear infection that prevented me from going in the water for a week. To keep me entertained, my mother took me to the movies—the same movie, playing at the local theater every day. I saw it five days in a row. To this day I can re-create many scenes in my memory, though I have not seen the movie in over sixty years. It was called *Stairway to Heaven*, with David Niven and Kim Hunter, about an RAF pilot who ditches his plane in the English Channel after a dogfight. He crashes, yet lives and tromps through the waves to the shore, where he meets Kim Hunter. They fall in love. There was an error in God's schedule. The airman was supposed to die. The rest of the movie consists of a courtroom trial held in heaven to decide whether the pilot should be allowed to remain with the living. In the end, he is saved by a tear shed by the woman he loves. Love conquers death.

The time of arrival.
The time of day.
The time of our lives.
The time of departure.
What were you saying?
The time of our lives.

The high sun blasts my boat. The air's a kiln. Uh-oh. Here comes global warming. The glacial ice melts in Antarctica. The Greenland ice has never melted, but it does now. The sea level rises. Drowned are the coasts of Louisiana. (I wouldn't sweat the oil.) Drowned Bangladesh. Venice was halfway there already. No more drinking water. No more London, Paris, or New York. Burble, burble. The canyons of the ocean deepen. Sharks patrol the sunken boulevards. Only the Sargasso Sea, where the horseshoe crabs go, and which receives no contributions from river water or melting ice, remains as it has always been. Remote. Self-sufficient. My kind of sea.

———

Sea. O.E. sæ "sheet of water, sea, lake," from P.Gmc. *saiwaz (cf. O.S. seo, O.Fris. se, M.Du. see), of unknown origin. Phrase sea change "transformation" is attested from 1610, first in Shakespeare (*The Tempest*, I.ii). Sea legs is from 1712; sea level first recorded 1806. At sea in the fig. sense of "perplexed" is attested from 1768, from lit. sense of "out of sight of land." At sea: lost.

———

Lately, I've been building a Lego rocket ship in the mornings and staring into space at night. I have been too long at sea, like one of the soprano-voiced English schoolboys, with curly blond hair, who apprentice themselves to short-tempered captains. Trouble is, I'm also the captain. These ought to be the calm years. I explode at trifles. I take it out on everyone. I leave keys in locks. How long does it take to come to terms with the facts of life? Whose child is shouting from the mudbank?

Between us, I wouldn't mind a little rough stuff. Mix it up with a jellyfish. Go three rounds with a Canada goose. If I can't find adversaries at sea, I'll take a shouting match with a cabdriver or a cop. He'd cuff me and take me down to the stationhouse. Book away, copper. You won't get a thing out of me. I'm no rat. Times, I walk the streets cruisin' for a bruisin'. I can be beaten senseless by every guy in this bar, and his girlfriend, and her newborn kitten. Remember the man in *The Pawnbroker* who pushed his hand down on the spike that held the store receipts? My, my. Such drama merely to retrieve memory and feel pain.

⌒

"The soul is our capacity for pain," said Marina Tsvetaeva. No wonder we spend so much time debating its existence.

———

All the photographs—on dressers, on desks and hall tables and side tables and bed tables, on the bookshelves, on the top bookshelf, and in the crevices between the books. All the photographs. Marble frames. Cheap plastic frames, like the frames in the old dime stores, with Natalie Wood's picture to make the frames more appealing. Drowned Natalie, looking forlorn and come-hither. What is one to do with so many photographs, relentlessly here? In lockets. On walls. The little tabletop barrels that project pictures on a loop. Here we are in Disney World. At the Grand Canyon. In the front yard. In the backyard. Beside the seaside, by the beautiful sea. You and me. Here I am. Here I am not. Verticals and horizontals. Ovals and squares. Eight-by-tens. Five-by-sevens. In artsy black and white and in living color. Framed in sterling silver and mounted on blocks of wood. Everyone makes wonderful photographs these days. Don't you think? The cameras are so good. You can't miss. All the photographs. Digital. Send. That one, for instance. So high the definition. So clear. Clearer than life.

———

A woman with green hair sticking straight in the air like sea grass has set up an easel on the east side of the creek. She waves, I wave back. My aunt Julia, who gave me the guitar, used to do that—sit on a hill overlooking a bay in Maine and paint. She used only oils and would set up her canvases and her easel, her tubes of paint, and her wood-and-canvas folding chair and re-create the view. When I was fifteen, I spent a week with her on one of her summer trips to Kennebunkport. It was a sign of what I thought of my aunt that I preferred being with her to being with my teenage friends. Julia was what people used to call an old maid, though she had a long-time boyfriend in the army who came and went. There was nothing old about her. She had no money. She worked as a secretary in a social club on St. Marks Place, where she lived her whole life in her parents' tenement apartment. Yet every winter she managed to scrounge up enough to take her to Palm Beach, to paint, and every summer she was painting in Kennebunkport. The owners of the B&Bs where she stayed charged her next to nothing. They liked having her around.

"Want to go to a drive-in?" she would ask. "Want to play checkers?" "Want to sit here and paint with me?"

She was very small and delicate, but her painting style was bold—brash colors and hard lines. When she grew old, she was bent with osteoporosis. She looked like a comma. Nothing affected her joie de vivre until the end. She spent her last weeks in a hospital, shouting sporadically in her sleep, great moaning shouts like keening. Over the years, she gave me some of her paintings, including a portrait of me by the bay in Maine. I do not know what happened to any of them.

In the Lower East Side tenements, whole families consisting of several generations lived and died in three rooms, maybe four. In one room, a midwife might be helping a young woman give birth, and the entire tenement would be filled with a baby's wailing. In another room, at exactly the same hour, a man might be dying in his bed. His family might be laying out his one dress suit for burial. What was it like for a child of, say, twelve, to wander between those two rooms? She probably would think nothing of it. That was just the way things were.

The separation of birth and death is fairly recent. The current distance between the events may serve to exaggerate the emotions attached to each. In my grandparents' day, the birth of a baby may not have engendered much fuss, the infant mortality rate among the poor being what it was. Death too may have been accepted as the predictable consequence of a hardscrabble life—though that might not have been true for a sudden death.

Lying on her back at night before sleep, in a room between the newborn and the dying, my imagined twelve-year-old most likely was thinking about boys, or that yellow dress in Wanamaker's, or about the Harold Lloyd movie she'd seen at Loew's Paradise that afternoon. Harold Lloyd on the skyscraper, as he hung for dear life from the scaffolding.

When I was writing in the war zones, I saw travel as akin to death. Death did not frighten me. I thought of it in a neutral way. I was leaving what was familiar for what was strange. The countries were strange. The customs were unknown, the language too. I might not ever return. I am hardly traveling such distances here on the creek, but some of the comparisons apply. I leave the shore to move about on uncertain ground. I am engulfed in mystery. I am on my own. The people I love, though only half a mile from here, feel far removed, as though I will never reach them again.

Cauterized memories. Too many. The terror and the sadness and the gunfire. It was practically all I saw of the world. Have you heard the one about the snail who knocked at a man's door? When the man opened it, he didn't see anyone except the snail, which he picked up and tossed into the bushes. One year later, the man heard a knock at his door. When he opened it this time, the snail said, "What was *that* about?" What was that about? My wife, my children, my friends, my work. What was that about? My accidental life.

The other day, I drove past a man waiting at a bus stop in East Quogue. He was grim-faced, like me—one of the Mexicans who do landscape and construction work around here. He wore overalls and a stained white dress shirt a few sizes too large. Many of the locals want to drive out the Mexicans, who, they say, are taking their jobs. But there is little work for anyone these days. I see the workers walking on the side of the highway carrying bags of groceries in both arms, or riding bikes too small for them. The man at the bus stop sat with his hands in his lap. As my car went by, he turned his head to follow my progress.

Water shines on rocks. Lustrous black gems. Black cur-raghs in Connemara. The sky's inflamed. My arms grow heavy. In "The Eye-Mote," Sylvia Plath wrote that what she wanted back was what she was before life locked her in a parenthesis. I paddle in my parenthesis. A red-and-orange balloon drifts overhead. It may have floated out of the hands of a little girl at the carnival that comes round here every summer. Up it goes—careless, bloodshot orange. A lift of a wave, a fall.

Here's an unusual fact: water is the earth's only self-renewing resource. It heals itself.

———

On the drive from Quogue to Bethesda last week, I found myself in a lane behind a car with a license plate that read WE PRAY. When the car peeled off, I was left behind a truck with a sign on the back that read RELIABLE CASKETS. As I approached Bethesda, I came upon a real estate sign that read ASK FOR AMY.

———

"Have you read *Many Lives, Many Masters*?" she asked. I said no. "When my father died," she said, "a half-dozen people, unconnected to one another, recommended it to me. I was at the dentist, and a dental hygienist who was working there only that one day, suggested that I read it."

"You believe in mystical things like that, don't you." I told her I found it uncharacteristic, since she was sensible and levelheaded in all other respects.

"I couldn't do my job if I didn't," she said. "The only news I would bring people in grief is that it will never be over. But that's why I thought you might be interested in *Many Lives, Many Masters*. It's about past lives and the continuity of our souls. And the author, Brian Weiss, was a skeptic, like you."

"I'm not a skeptic. I don't believe in that stuff at all," I said.

"That's not true. In *Making Toast*, you made the point of telling us that you felt a comforting pat on your forearm."

"But I dismissed it as a twitch."

"But you mentioned it, which means you did not dismiss it. And it was telling that Ginny did not feel the patting. And she wasn't looking in your direction when it happened. Because Ginny doesn't need proof of Amy's presence. She feels it all around her."

"I do not."

"I think you will, sooner or later, for the same reason I could not do my kind of work if I didn't believe in 'that stuff.'"

"You're talking about God."

"Not necessarily," she said.

"That's good, because I already believe in God. I just don't like him."

"But he . . ."

"Don't say it."

She laughed. "Read the book anyway. You're looking to get Amy back."

"If a book could do that . . ."

———

Hilarious, touching, silly—how many people believe in the tactile presence of the dead. I prefer traditional magic and hocus-pocus—soothsayers, tarot cards, nothing up my sleeve. I liked it better in the old movies when Abbott and Costello were chased by ghosts, and mediums ran séances on a wet afternoon, faking the voices of the departed and fleecing the suckers. The village of Lily Dale, New York, has a certain morbid charm. The entire population consists of mediums. It was founded shortly after the Civil War, and mothers and fathers of dead soldiers would come to Lily Dale to speak with their sons. I don't know who goes there today. There really is no need. Books on communicating with the dead seem to have overtaken the spooky trade. They have figured death out. One book I looked at reworked Purgatory into an idea called "the waiting room of the soul." I hope they have *Playboy*.

The books are fun to read. I'll bet they were fun to write, too—at least up to the point where the author began to believe in his own poppycock. There was a man on TV some years ago, an earnest, self-confident sort, who built a popular show on his ability to communicate with "the other side." If the dead could speak, why would they choose *him*? A simple trust in invisible things should be enough, surely, without the need to talk with the dead. At the O.J. trial, in regard to the question of Simpson's presence at the murder scene, the prosecution held that the absence of evidence did not constitute evidence of absence. The visible invisible. Like love, I suppose. Like absence itself. You can see absence in the face of someone who feels it.

—

For my "If you say so" file—an interview with Dr. Masaru Emoto, author of *The Message from Water*, conducted by Reiko Myamoto Dewey, who has a website called The Spirit of Ma'at.

REIKO: You mentioned in your book how you would type out words on a piece of paper and paste these written words onto a bottle, and see how the water reacted to the words. . . . Have you come across a particular word or phrase in your research that you have found to be most helpful in cleaning up the natural waters of the world?

DR. EMOTO: Yes. There is a special combination that seems

to be perfect for this, which is *love* plus the combination of thanks and appreciation reflected in the English word *gratitude*. . . . Love is an active word and gratitude is passive.

REIKO: Would you tell us . . . what you believe these water crystals really are?

DR. EMOTO: When ice melts, the crystalline structure becomes an illusion. It's there—and yet it's not there, because you can no longer see it. . . . In Buddhism, we talk about attaining sattori, or reaching enlightenment. People who attain sattori do not become ghosts. They are able to achieve a certain stage of development at the soul level and return to God for a while before they move on to their next assignment. . . .

REIKO: So when a person dies, if they are unable to attain sattori at that time, their soul remains on this planet as water?

DR. EMOTO: That is what I believe, yes.

———

Gödel shook up mathematics when he said there are some truths that never can be proven as true. You can give yourself a fine old headache working this out. But let's say you're a math dummy like me, and you accept Gödel without proof and concede there are things we can never know. That doesn't take the wonder out of math. Numbers make the world go round. Mathematical calculations, including those even I can do, require no negotiations, no international summit. Two plus three equals five, in Akron and in Tehran. The equation unites those places by that agreement. Sufficiently wondrous, if you ask me.

⁓

As if that were possible. As if we actually believed in a world of possibilities. As if we did not know everything before we had knowledge of it. As if we needed to fall in love or to burn our fingers on the potbellied stove or to see that saltwater cordgrass or that slice of sea lettuce as if for the first time, when we have lived with it in our imagined seas all our imagined lives. As if they meant it when they offered a penny for my thoughts. As if they couldn't read my mind.

The trouble with hardening one's heart—as God found out when he toyed with Pharaoh—is not that one's heart turns to stone, but that the stone endures. I have all the wrong feelings.

⁓

My therapist friend refers to *Making Toast* as a sort of guide and corrective to my current state of mind. This feels strange to me. When you've written and published a book, it goes out like a child sent out into the world. When you reread it, it seems as if it were written by someone else, which is true, since, like a creek, we move on naturally. The other day I was in a lecture hall, about to give a reading of *Making Toast*, and the man who introduced me told the audience that he was impressed with the book's sure commitment to life. I could not look up at him when he was speaking of me, because I know I am weaker than my book.

⁓

The characters in a novel I'm writing have lost control of themselves. The one-eyed hag has become a two-legged dog, with a red cart fastened to its ass. The gatekeeper has become a beekeeper. He's so out of things, he tries to open and close a gate made of bees. He drinks. The hero of the piece is spread in a hundred directions like the roots of an old tree. As for the villains, there are so many by now, I'd be better off yoking them under a single name. This is what happens when you do not pay attention to the novels you write. Oh yes. And Death. A character called Death has stuck his Roman nose into the plot. He plays a vampire who needs a transfusion. It's a bad idea, don't you think? To give a transfusion to a vampire?

I sometimes wish I owned a shop instead, where I sold coconuts or objets d'art or bowie knives—anything but books. People would come to my shop to get the things they want. And I would give them what they want, and we both would take satisfaction in the transaction. The trouble with writing is that you give people what they don't want, and by the time they realize they needed what you gave them, they have forgotten where your shop is located. You, meanwhile, never noticed them in the first place. You were intent on your work, which consists of patricide and theft. I read Cavafy the other day, cover to cover, with every intent of robbing his grave.

There's only one point to writing. It allows you to do impossible things. Sure, most of the time it's chimney sweeping and dung removal. Or plastering. A lot of the time, writing is plastering or caulking or pointing up the bricks. But every so often there is a moment in the dead of morning when everything is still as starlight and something invades your room, like a bird that has flown through the window, and you are filled with as much joy as panic. And then you think: I can do anything.

I told a class of mine: writing makes sorrow endurable, evil intelligible, justice desirable, and love possible. I talk the talk.

And love possible? At least I will not be like Emerson two years after the death of his son, Waldo. Emerson's reaction to Waldo's death in his essay "Experience" is shocking. He calls grief nothing deeper than a mood—"scene painting and counterfeit." He did not always think so. In "Threnody," the poem written soon after Waldo's death, you can practically hear the author tear at his garments, so stricken is he with his loss. But later, in "Experience," he has steeled himself in the name of some higher truth and superior thought. "The only thing grief has taught me," he writes, "is to know how shallow it is." Colder still: "In the death of my son, now more than two years ago, I seem to have lost a beautiful estate,—no more. I cannot get it nearer to me. . . . I grieve that grief can teach me nothing, nor carry me one step into real nature."

So keen is he not to feel his son's death, so intent on turning his individual stoicism into general philosophy, one cannot help but wonder what sort of father Emerson was. But that is none of my business. Either he means his denial of emotion or he does not. And if he means it, his essay, so contemptuous of grief, comes as a slap in the face. There is an odd logic at work here. People in grief become more like themselves. Precisely. Emerson was always craning his neck toward the clouds. He was born to dwell in abstraction. Given that, he is perfectly, exquisitely more like himself in grief—too lofty for pain. Not I. Yet what should one make of one's grief?

———

Love is heaven and heaven is love.

—SIR WALTER SCOTT, QUOTED IN *STAIRWAY TO HEAVEN*

———

For some seven hours now I have been out here. I could go the whole day, into the evening and the night. I am not alone, after all. The sky and the water are with me. The insects and the birds. They are with me impersonally. See that thrush half hidden in a tangle of leaves? The red berry beside it? And that yellow wildflower? And that one? Hardly alone. What am I trying to recall?

———

In Hong Kong, I interviewed a teenage boy named Khu, who had escaped from Haiphong by hopping a junk at night. His mother and father were dead. He had no one else he was close to. The junk he boarded carried thirteen other escapees. It was thirteen meters long. They were fifty-two days at sea, supplied with only twenty kilos of rice and forty liters of water. When the food ran out, some of the men on the boat quarreled over the fish they caught. The boat captain had them killed. The number of passengers was down to six. When again there was no food, the captain decided to kill Khu.

"The boat master told a boy who was a neighbor of mine to take a hammer and hit me on the head, so that they might eat my flesh," Khu told me. His friend informed him of the plot.

One night, when they thought he was sleeping, the men draped a shirt over Khu's head and hit him with a piece of metal. They lifted the shirt, and Khu was crying. They let him live. Khu said he understood how men could do such things, if they were desperate.

"Then would you kill a child in order to survive?" I asked him.

"No," he said. "We go together in one boat. I would not kill in order to live."

At dusk, we stood together by a chain-link fence, overlooking Hong Kong Harbor and a windfall of lights. "What do you think about when you look at Hong Kong?" I asked him.

"I see lots of lights, which are beautiful. And boats."

"What do you think when you look at the boats?"
"The boats have lights, which are also beautiful."
"What else is beautiful, Khu?"
He answered quietly. "Everything is beautiful."

———

Beauty addresses itself chiefly to sight; but there
is a beauty for the hearing too, as in certain
combinations of words and in all kinds of music,
for melodies and cadences are beautiful; and minds
that lift themselves above the realm of sense to a
higher order are aware of the beauty in the conduct
of life, in actions, in character, in the pursuits of the
intellect; and there is the beauty of the virtues.

—PLOTINUS, *THE ENNEADS*

———

Am I wrong about the power of confinement? Half wrong,
I think. The breath of this world will not be contained. A
lifer I spoke with in Attica thumbtacked "Invictus" to his
cell wall. At a poetry reading in Moscow, I sat in a crowd of
fifteen thousand who had come to catch the poet's subversive
allusions. The Cambodian children performed folk dances
on the dirt floor in the refugee camp near a tall stack of

prosthetic limbs. After the funeral of one of their own, the Sudanese boys stood together and sang.

One night, in Sunset Park, Brooklyn, a sixteen-year-old Puerto Rican girl gave me a walking tour of the neighborhood. She used to coat her fingernails with lacquer, to harden them for gang fights. In the fall, she was going to enter college. Her father, a drunk, beat her and her sisters and their mother. When we went back to her two-room apartment, only her sisters were there. She laughed to cheer them up and introduced me: "This is your real father."

I keep their letters in one very large blue shopping bag and four smaller shopping bags, near my desk. Many I have answered. Most I have not. I lack the heart. Why I don't throw them out, I do not know. What help can I possibly bring to anyone? It gets so that I flinch at the post office when I see a letter from a stranger. They are handwritten. The hand is often shaky. The stationery is formal, to befit the occasion, mine and theirs. Blue stationery. Beige and cream color. When the stationery was purchased originally, the people who write to me now felt that they were establishing themselves in their neighborhoods, in their communities. They were becoming substantial. They had their own stationery, with their names in embossed lettering. We did that, too. We got formal stationery for the New Hampshire farmhouse. The paper was more substantial than the house. But that was the point. That was the front. Off-white stationery with embossed blue lettering, to certify our lives.

———

Everybody grieves. I see grief in their faces. I do not need their letters to know it. I do not create their grief out of mine. To each his own. Their messages are brine-soaked. They wind up flotsam. No one reads them, not even in Atlantis. Everybody grieves. The faraway look. The bowed head and stooped walk. One could see life as nothing but grief. The brave processions in the street. The buried eyes. Bright buried eyes.

Into every heartbreak beauty intrudes.

Lilies in a potter's field.

Everybody graves.

———

For Graves' disease, I take 10 mg of Tapazole twice a day, along with atenolol, a beta-blocker. The slowness of the cure tries my patience. I have been nearly three months with this disease, but I am stronger than I was several weeks ago. Otherwise I could not be out here. The pills must be working.

As I understand it, this is what is happening inside me: my thyroid is spewing hormones. The Tapazole works the way the equipment in the Gulf is supposed to work. It caps and contains the thyroid. The body metabolizes the spilled hormones. I am a little Gulf made cunningly.

⁓

"When things level off in your system," said the doctor, "I'll give you a radioactive iodine pill."

"What'll it do?"

"Destroy the thyroid, or most of it, which absorbs the iodine in your system now."

"What happens to the homeless iodine?"

"You piss it away. After that, I'll give you another pill, Synthroid, which is chemically identical to the thyroid."

"A whole systemic change. What will I feel?"

"Nothing. Like most systemic changes, you'll be one way one day, another the next."

⁓

At home with James the other day, I sat on the couch watching a documentary on the life of Roberto Clemente. James sat on the floor a few feet away, playing with a large-piece jigsaw puzzle of Lightning McQueen, the racing car of the animated movie. The piece on Clemente was about his three thousandth hit, but it also emphasized his character and generosity. "If you have the chance to help someone and you do not take it," he said, "you are wasting your time on earth." A moment later, James asked, "Will you help me, Boppo?" James did most of the puzzle himself, but when Lightning McQueen was complete, several of the pieces kept sliding out of their slots. Frustrated and overtired, James swung his arms and scattered the pieces around the room. First he blamed me. Then the puzzle. "Stupid puzzle!" he shouted. "Stupid stupid stupid puzzle!" Then he sobbed in my arms.

That night I lay down with him in his bed. He always asks me to stay with him until he falls asleep. As we lay side by side in silence, I felt his little hand touch my forearm and rest there. His body twitched, indicating that he was sleeping. I remained with him.

⁓

When you are out alone in a kayak, you need a plan if you capsize. The most difficult rescue technique is the Eskimo roll, which requires turning the boat over completely, submerging yourself with the boat on top of you, and then resurfacing. I have never tried it, though the more I go kayaking, the likelier it is that I'll use the technique. The instructional books stress the need to maintain stability in a boat. The forces of buoyancy and gravity are equalized when the boat is at rest. The books also point out that capsizing does not occur only in rapids or rough waters. What they call "drowning traps" exist in the calmest creek. I imagine that the worst moment in the Eskimo roll occurs when you're upside down holding your breath and cannot believe you will ever sit up straight again.

I turn. It turns. The kayak creates a little wake. I swerve. It swerves. I move with it. It moves with me. Viewed from the side we look like a single entity—a man from his head to the base of his torso, which then seems to splay into two very long legs, one fore, one aft. Or an upside-down umbrella, with me as the handle. Or a demitasse cup and saucer, with me as the cup. The boat fits. It makes sense. It is my slot. I am its piece.

Near noon. About now they return from the beach. The kids hose off their legs. Jessie has brought in seashells, which she adds to her collection on a plate in the kitchen. Nate has fallen asleep under the beach umbrella. Wendy carries him upstairs to continue his nap. Sammy, James, Andrew, and Ryan play Wiffle ball on the front lawn with Carl, John, and Harris. Ginny sets the table for lunch and wonders how long I'll be out here. She stops and looks up from her work, as if she has heard someone call her name.

On the creek, the birds too hesitate. Customarily they seem all flight and motion, yet like everyone, they come to a dead stop from time to time, deciding where to go next. You see them clearly when they hesitate—the cocked head of the egret, the glazed eyes. A taxidermist's dream, they pause between the past and something else. You can say they are only themselves when they use their wings, but they are no less birds in this. The bird who hesitates is not lost. I watch them, still as an egret.

———

I have submitted to a new control:
A power is gone, which nothing can restore;
A deep distress hath humanized my soul.
—WORDSWORTH, "ELEGIAC STANZAS"

———

The lifer in Attica told me, "I don't think anything that has been created can be destroyed." Lewis Thomas, the philosopher-physician, said the closest he could come to be-lieving in an afterlife was the fact that nothing in nature disappears. If this is so, does it irritate Death? So little power after all, except to break our hearts.

So I burst into the bank, a Glock in each fist, and yelled, "Nobody move!" Nobody did. Because no one was in the bank. And it wasn't a bank. It was a field of malting barley that extended a hundred hectares in every direction. And the wind picked up the torn end of the field and folded it over me, like a duvet or a shroud.

"Don't you feel the perfect fool now," said Death. Now and forever.

⁓

Death is soundproof. Silence unspeakable. I am part of the silence in my silence.

The heart yearns in silence. The mind rages in silence. Decides in silence. Betrays in silence. The conscience roils, plots, lies in silence. In silence, the rumination, the medita-tion, the vow. We search in silence. War in silence. Regret in silence. Love. We love in silence. Think of that.

⁓

Water heals itself. Am I the dead one? If I am dead, I am unable to lie down, which would suggest I am not dead. I am alive with memory. I can weep. And I can praise.

These ducks, for example, in arrowhead formations over the Atlantic. And the Atlantic herself that gushes in the half-light. And the beach that contorts to shapes of angels on tombstones, awls, hunchbacks, lovers lying thigh to thigh. And the driftwood from a mackerel schooner that still bears the stench of the catch. And the trees that stand together like farmhands on a break. And the slant of the sky. And the shingles of the sky. And a cloud like Tennessee. And this creek. And this small boat. And my living. And my dead. *Ave.*

Our daughter dies and there are those who carried her. I shall die and there will be those who carry me. On and on, down the cobblestones of the village, through the swales of the dunes. On and on we bear one another into the bruise-dark waters. The burden of the generations. The burden of burdens. Past the heaving rib cage and the bloodshot eye. Remembering, forgetting, and remembering again. We are what we never were. Hardly alone.

You never let a stranger feel unwelcome or out of place. You never deserted anyone in need. You loved. You gave whatever you had to give. You never wasted anything, especially your life. You healed. You lessened pain. You skipped stones on the water. You loved. You loved shoes. You loved coffee. You loved fancy old restaurants. You loved walks. You loved dogs. You loved jigsaw puzzles. You glowed when you held your children in your arms. You glowed in your wedding dress. You comforted. You protected. You loved. You tossed your head back when you laughed. You smiled when you swam. You loved. When you were five, you stood on my shoes as we danced. You made two syllables of "Dad." The day you were born, I carried you home. You were an ocean in my arms.

At the end of the morning, everything is calm and slow moving. I feel the cold breath of the sea. A transparent worm disappears into a wave. A great blue heron parks itself on a dock across the canal and looks seaward, as if trying to remember something. There is just enough wind to make one appreciate it. Fish, caught and released, nurse their bloodless wounds.

Let the shiners chatter. Let the wind touch me. Let the crabs hide. Let the mussels hide. Let the jellyfish bloom. Let the clouds shift. Let the ripples from a small boat embrace the waters of the world.

———

Everything disappears and nothing disappears. In the late 1970s, the government of Argentina imprisoned, tortured, and killed tens of thousands of men, women, and children, so-called enemies of the state. They were snatched off the streets and never seen again, thus the name given them, the "desaparecidos." Every Thursday, the wives and mothers of the desaparecidos walked in circles around the Plaza de Mayo, carrying photographs of their sons, daughters, and husbands swinging on chains from their necks, like good-luck charms, presenting unassailable proof to anyone who cared to look that the subjects of the photo did, at one time, exist. Love makes for tenacious detectives. The Argentine mothers were not patrolling the Plaza de Mayo in the name of revolutionary ideas, but because they missed those they love.

———

Speed Vogel died at age ninety, six months after Amy. I knew him only slightly, though his wife, Lou Ann Walker, is a long-time friend. By the time I met Speed, his mind and body were going, and he moved about in a wheelchair maneuvered by

Lou Ann. She was a good deal younger than Speed, but they had a long, lovely marriage, and a beautiful daughter, Kate. I watched Lou Ann as she looked after Speed in his last years—how careful and tender she was with him. He would blurt out Tourette's-like bursts and plaintive cries, and she would touch him gently and soothe him, as one would a spooked horse. She brought him with her everywhere. One night she was giving a reading from her novel in progress. She had barely begun to speak when Speed issued an anguished shout from his seat. Lou Ann laid her novel on the lectern, went to him, and whispered in his ear. When he was calm, she returned to her reading. Everyone in the hall observed her with sadness and admiration, knowing that we were getting a lesson in what it means to love someone all the time.

———

"So what did you think of the book?" she asked.

"When Weiss tries to formalize his feelings and make them into a theory, he's weak. But I was surprised how much I took to the spiritual part."

"Past lives?"

"He said something when he was first aware of the presiding presence of the dead—'Beneath my chill, I felt a great love stirring.'"

"Do you feel anything like that?" She studied my confusion. "Why did you write *Making Toast*?"

"It was therapy. As long as I was writing about Amy, I could keep her alive."

"What about afterwards?"

"When the book was finished, it was as if she had died again."

"The book isn't enough," she said.

"No, it's not enough."

"So what do you do now? Write another book?"

"There has to be something more lasting than a book."

"And what would that be?"

⸺

Last night Ginny ordered candles. I watched her through the opening of one room into another. She spoke into the phone and asked the man in the candle shop if he had a certain candle she likes, with a four-inch diameter. As she spoke, she was standing beside a lit candle in a brass holder and was illuminated by its flickering light. On the wall behind her was the seascape I had bought her in SoHo. Through the window the setting sun flecked part of the painting with patches of gold, which looked like candles in the water. Ginny's voice was soft, as it always is. Evidently the candle shop had the ones she wanted. I did not realize that she knew I was observing her. But just then she looked at me and smiled.

———

And love possible.

———

I remember now. It was on the beach. And we were there, all of us intact. And I was holding Jessie's hand at the lip of the ocean. "Here comes a wave. There it goes. Will it touch our knees or our ankles or our toes?" And Jessie squealed, "Our toes!" And above us, perched on the dune, was Amy, smiling. She was watching Jessie and me, and she was happy.

———

> I am in a mind to bless. Blessed be the book, the
> page, the verse, the word, the letter. Blessed be the
> great names and the ungreat names. Blessed be
> the velvet that is the color of wine, and the wine.
> Blessed be the particle in the light, and the light.
> Blessed be the shoulder and blessed be the burden.
> Blessed be the calendar. Blessed be the clock.
>
> —LEON WIESELTIER, *KADDISH*

Nothing of him that doth fade,
But doth suffer as a sea-change
Into something rich and strange.
—SHAKESPEARE, *THE TEMPEST*

Drifting again, I look down into the water of my birth, of our birth—the fluid in our bodies, the salt of our blood. A white gull poses on the dock of the Yacht Club, fresh as a girl. A blue claw crab settles on a stone at the base of the dock. He is done with prowling for a while. A dubious duck treads on a gray slab on the shore above, its brown-and-gray down lifted by a breeze. A dragonfly threads a course among the reeds. My hands close on the air, in an unconscious prayer.

In every heartbreak beauty intrudes. I am willing to be taken. The wind touches my wrists. I hear the caterwauling of the crows. I taste and smell the clammy air. I see everything. Art does not make up a life. Experience does not make up a life. And death does not make up a life either. I don't see why eternity has to last forever. Those whom I have loved and who have loved me—no matter what happened to dilute that love or to cool it or even to drown it: I should like to gather them all on that far shore and thank them. They were my life.

———

Love conquers death. No celestial jury will bring Amy back to me. I will not see her either, no matter how others may want me to. She will not talk to me. But in the time since she died, I have been aware, every minute, of my love for her. She lives in my love. This morning when I climbed into my kayak and headed out, I knew that I would be going no-where, as I have been going nowhere for the past two and a half years. But my love for my daughter makes somewhere out of nowhere. In this boat, on this creek, I am moving forward, even as I am moving in circles. Amy returns in my love, alive and beautiful. I have her still.

———

> **Grief.** The state of mind brought about when love, having lost to death, learns to breathe beside it. See also love.

———

I aim my boat toward the shore.